Second Edition

CUSTOMER SERVICE
A PRACTICAL APPROACH

Elaine K. Harris

Tulsa Community College

Prentice Hall
Upper Saddle River, New Jersey 07458

ication Data

Harris, Elaine K.
    Customer service : a practical approach / Elaine K. Harris.
        p.   cm.
    Includes bibliographical references and index.
    ISBN 0-13-082665-0
    1. Customer services.   I. Title.
    HF5415.5.H2897   2000
    658.8' 12—dc21

                                            99-21221
                                               CIP

For John, Kendall, and Andrew,
who bring special joy to my life

Acquisitions Editor: *Elizabeth Sugg*
Editorial Assistant: *Delia Uherec*
Director of Production and Manufacturing: *Bruce Johnson*
Managing Editor: *Mary Carnis*
Editorial/Production Supervision: *WordCrafters Editorial Services, Inc.*
Manufacturing Manager: *Marc Bove*
Marketing Manager: *Shannon Simonsen*
Composition: *BookMasters, Inc.*
Cover printer: *Victor Graphics, Inc.*
Printer/binder: *Victor Graphics, Inc.*

© 2000, 1996 by Prentice-Hall, Inc.
Upper Saddle River, New Jersey 07458

Printed in the United States of America

10 9 8 7 6 5 4 3

ISBN 0-13-082665-0

PRENTICE-HALL INTERNATIONAL (UK) LIMITED, *London*
PRENTICE-HALL OF AUSTRALIA PTY. LIMITED, *Sydney*
PRENTICE-HALL CANADA INC., *Toronto*
PRENTICE-HALL HISPANOAMERICANA, S.A., *Mexico*
PRENTICE-HALL OF INDIA PRIVATE LIMITED, *New Delhi*
PRENTICE-HALL OF JAPAN, INC., *Tokyo*
SIMON & SCHUSTER ASIA PTE. LTD., *Singapore*
EDITORA PRENTICE-HALL DO BRASIL, LTDA., *Rio de Janeiro*

CONTENTS

ABOUT THE AUTHOR

Elaine Harris grew up in Bartlesville, Oklahoma, and graduated from the University of Oklahoma with a Bachelor of Science in Arts and Sciences, majoring in Fashion Merchandising. The following year she graduated from the University of Central Oklahoma with her Master of Education degree in Adult and Secondary Education, majoring in Marketing Education.

Elaine has extensive experience in retail and retail management, and began her teaching experience at Oklahoma Junior College in Tulsa, Oklahoma. In 1988 she began teaching Marketing and Fashion Merchandising at Tulsa Junior College in Tulsa, Oklahoma. The Tulsa marketplace began to attract jobs in the area of customer service and saw numerous call centers open for business. Elaine researched and created, with industry support, the Customer Service Program at Tulsa Community College. This program has assisted in the training of hundreds of customer-focused employees in the Tulsa metropolitan area. Elaine has served on several city and regional task forces to identify the training needs and to develop appropriate training to meet the growing customer service employee needs. Elaine is a frequent guest speaker and trainer in the areas of customer service and marketing throughout the region.

When she is not writing or teaching, Elaine stays busy with her two young children. She is also an encourager to her husband in his growing telecommunications management consulting business, Harris, Skrivan, and Associates.

Customer service is an integral part of doing business. Today's customer service providers must have adequate preparation to interact effectively with today's customers. This preparation is the result of a commitment to increased understanding of the customer service industry, the knowledge of current trends, the ability to interpret those trends, and the development of the fundamental skills necessary to achieve excellence.

A new generation of customer service providers is emerging. This new generation is excited about what they can offer their customers and how they can help their organizations to accomplish goals. They eagerly accept the challenge of expanding their understanding of the business world. These customer service providers are well educated, open to new ideas, adaptable, and motivated; they possess superior communication skills and have an enlightened understanding of the multicultural marketplace in which business is conducted. Technology is a tool to more effectively meet the ever-changing needs of customers The desire for additional knowledge reflects a commitment to personal and professional growth.

In response to the need for increased customer service and for qualified customer service professionals, *Customer Service: A Practical Approach* was created. Those with a desire to develop an increased knowledge of key concepts in customer service will benefit from the organized and concise layout. This publication is unique because it allows the reader to examine the dynamics of the customer service industry while also providing exercises to develop the skills necessary to compete. It transcends superficial elements and focuses on the skills and strategies that lead to successful implementation of customer service.

Customer Service: A Practical Approach tackles the important issues facing customer service providers and customer service managers today. Individual success is contingent on how effectively fundamental skills are mastered and carried out. In addition to important content, special emphasis is placed on self-assessment and the mastery of those skills and abilities that are missing from the average employee's resume. Today's workforce must continue to improve upon the skills that provide tangible evidence of individual and corporate productivity.

Chapter 1 answers the question, "What is customer service?" The concept of satisfaction is explained and the reasons that excellent customer service is so rare are explored. All customers have needs that they consider extremely important. Providers must have the ability to assess customer needs and begin the process of need satisfaction.

In Chapter 2 the barriers to customer service are explained. Some of the most obvious barriers to the provision of excellent customer service are within the control of the customer service provider. How do businesses begin to understand the expectations and perceptions that their customers bring into a customer/provider relationship? Reputation management describes the attempt to identify how a company is perceived and establishes an action plan to follow to maintain or enhance the reputation of the business.

Customer service is a common topic of discussion, but it is surprising how little focused attention is directed toward the actual accomplishment of customer satisfaction. Credibility is crucial as we interact with our internal and external customers, but conveying credibility is not always easy. By following basic tips for conveying credibility, customer service providers can actively express believability and professionalism.

Creative problem solving skills assist those interacting with customers to determine appropriate solutions to challenges. The role of problem solving in customer service is explored in Chapter 3. Customer service providers need to be equipped with an active understanding of how to work through problems and how to choose effective solutions.

Chapter 4 defines what a strategy is and examines how a well-developed strategy can provide opportunities for customer service excellence. The role of infrastructure is explained and the reader is challenged to identify infrastructure requirements that are not being met. If an appropriate infrastructure is not in place, customer service goals will not be met, regardless of how much providers want to provide excellent service. Understanding the concept of creating a customer service culture can provide employees with a positive work environment that encourages excellent customer service. When developing a strategy, providers must establish goals, divide customers into serviceable groups, make plans, and define a timetable for evaluation.

We hear a considerable amount of talk about the importance of empowerment, yet surprisingly, few managers really know what it means and know how to empower their employees. Chapter 5 explains how empowerment can positively impact a provider's ability to serve the customer. Customers can participate in providing their own customer service, and frequently want to be involved in the process. Systems must be designed so that customer service is allowed to happen. All too often, the very companies that claim to give the best service are in reality not providing it and could not provide it no matter how hard they try. Why? Because the systems they have in place do not encourage customer service.

Chapter 6 defines what communication is and how effective communication can enhance customer relations. Customer intelligence can assist organizations in recognizing how best to communicate with customers and how to develop a foundation of understanding of the business. Most customer service situations require superior listening skills. The proper voice inflection can enable individuals to convey messages in a more professional manner, and by using appropriate words the customer service provider's message can be both positive and professional. Technology has significantly impacted the world of communications. New technological opportunities can enhance productivity and result in increased accuracy.

Everyone has at some time encountered a "challenging" individual. Chapter 7 looks at who those challenging customers are. In a unique approach, 10 characteristics of challenging customers are explained. Helpful suggestions for positive interaction and techniques for challenge resolution are provided. Empathy and respect play an important role in relating to our challenging customers, but the ability to express empathy and show respect is not instinctive.

Customer service can be a very rewarding profession, but frequently individuals must find their own motivation as they pursue the rewards. Self-esteem varies from one individual to another. Chapter 8 explains what motivation is and offers suggestions for self-motivation and techniques for motivating others. Some of the keys to increased motivation are focusing on past successes, taking care of ourselves, practicing teamwork, and spending time with positive people. Other keys to increased motivation reveal that the opportunities for motivation are largely within each individual's control.

The most recognizably outstanding companies are known for their excellent leadership. The leaders of an organization have the ability to create an interdependent culture that continually reminds employees that aspiring to success is a group activity. Chapter 9 profiles the characteristics of excellent leaders and stresses the benefits of goal setting. New-generation leaders are designing new methods to reinforce training to benefit both employees and customers.

The fact that it is much more costly to attract new customers than it is to maintain current customers has been recognized for many years. In spite of this knowledge, numerous organizations have had few formal programs in place to keep customers active. Chapter 10 explains the concepts of customer retention, churn, defection rate, and customer lifetime value, the chapter describes how to tell if you need to improve your customer retention program and how to establish a customer retention program. The periodic measurement of customers' satisfaction keeps customer retention programs on target.

Keeping up with and delivering customer service to the changing marketplace is the focus of Chapter 11. New technologies are emerging and customers are using them to enhance the ease with which they conduct their daily lives. This raises the expectation of how the customer service industry will respond to customers. The growth of call centers, the Internet, and e-mail all indicate that customers want to use these growing innovations and that they want to be served through them also.

Chapter 12 wraps the topics of Chapter 1 to 11 together and challenges the reader to continue the process of seeking excellence in customer service.

In addition to the major chapter topics, chapters are introduced with a special "Remember This" quotation that relates to the chapter content. Chapters conclude with review questions to reinforce the concepts discussed in each chapter, and Skill Building exercises furnish the opportunity to develop the important skills necessary to become an excellent customer service provider. Periodic Challenges provide unique experiences in special customer service areas.

Customer Service: A Practical Approach goes beyond explaining why customer service is important by defining proven methods for creating an environment that achieves excellence in customer service.

ACKNOWLEDGMENTS

Special thanks to my parents, Don and Shirley Seizinger, who taught me the importance of serving others, and for always being there when I need them. Thanks to Rebecca Legleiter, my wonderful colleague who provides words of encouragement and who challenges me to think of new methods of instructional delivery. Thanks to the hundreds of customer service and marketing students that I have been blessed with over the years. Many of their stories and examples are shared in these pages.

Thanks to my friends, Sharon Myers, Shelly Drullinger, Jody Schneeberg, Kristi Reid, Kim Lewis and my brother Karl Seizinger, for being cherished encouragers. Special appreciation to Pam and Bonnie Baird who enabled me to coordinate the many demands of my life and whose daily encouragement is a blessing. Most of all thank you to my husband, John, and my children, Kendall and Andrew, the most important customers in my life.

Finally, I would like to thank Prentice Hall for supporting this project—Specifically, Elizabeth Sugg for believing in this publication enough to take it to a second edition, and Tally Morgan for creating a visually appealing document from my words.

WHAT IS CUSTOMER SERVICE?

- **CUSTOMER SERVICE IS IMPORTANT!**
- **WHAT IS CUSTOMER SERVICE?**
- **UNDERSTANDING OF SATISFACTION**
- **WHY IS EXCELLENT CUSTOMER SERVICE SO RARE?**
- **FIVE NEEDS OF EVERY CUSTOMER**
- **EXTERNAL AND INTERNAL CUSTOMERS**
- **COST OF LOSING A CUSTOMER**
- **SKILL BUILDING: "MY CUSTOMER"**
- **CHALLENGE 1: WRITING COMPLIMENT/COMPLAINT LETTERS**
- **OPPORTUNITIES FOR CRITICAL THINKING**

REMEMBER THIS

A customer is the most important visitor on our premises. He is not dependent on us; we are dependent on him. He is not an interruption in our work; he is the purpose of it. He is not an outsider in our business; he is part of it. We are not doing him a favor by serving him; he is doing us a favor by giving us an opportunity to do so.

MAHATMA GANDHI

CUSTOMER SERVICE IS IMPORTANT!

One of the most effective and least expensive ways to market a business is through excellent customer service. Customers are an obvious requirement for doing business. The importance of customer service is at an all-time high. Businesses realize that providing a product or service alone is not enough in today's competitive economic environment.

Today, customers are much more sophisticated than they were even five years ago. They are informed about how products should perform and know that if they are dissatisfied with the service that they receive, someone else probably sells the product and will provide better service. They may also expect that expressing their unhappiness with a situation will elicit a positive result.

Customer service is in style! People are talking about its importance, and they go into the marketplace expecting to receive it. The provision of customer service is an important component of the business cycle. In many cases, customer service is the positive element that keeps current business coming back. The customer service provider is frequently the one who "saves the day" and the account.

When a person goes out of his or her way to provide excellent customer service, work is more fun and more fulfilling; as a result, positive relationships with others develop.

WHAT IS CUSTOMER SERVICE?

Shockingly, the average customer service provider doesn't know! *Customer service is anything we do for the customer that enhances the customer experience.* Customers have varying ideas of what they expect from customer interaction. The customer service provider must get to know his or her customers and strive to provide them with excellent customer service. No matter how accurately we see our definition of customer service, we still have to live up to what our customer thinks that customer service is. The customer's satisfaction is the goal to attain.

UNDERSTANDING OF SATISFACTION

Customer satisfaction is the customer's overall feeling of contentment with a customer interaction. Customer satisfaction recognizes the difference between customer expectations and customer perceptions. Satisfaction may develop quickly or it may be cultivated over a period of time. Customers have many concerns, and our job is to reduce as much of the customer's stress as possible and to create a pleasant customer experience, while also providing current information and helping to solve problems for the customer. Satisfaction may be a customer's afterthought. The customer may think back on the experience and realize how pleasant or unpleasant it was.

EXAMPLES OF CUSTOMER SERVICE

1. Free car wash with fill-up
2. Calling the customer by name

3. Easy return policy
4. Updated map of the area in rental cars
5. A doctor calling you back to see how you are feeling after a professional visit
6. On-time delivery
7. Courtesy
8. Enthusiasm
9. Showing the customer that you care
10. Excellent follow-up
11. Empathy in handling customer complaints and questions
12. Well-explained instructions
13. Illustrations of encouragement
14. Suggesting a less expensive option
15. Package carry-out

WHY IS EXCELLENT CUSTOMER SERVICE SO RARE?

Customer service is rare because it requires two things that the average person and organization are unwilling to commit to: spending money and taking action. In business today everyone is talking about how important customer service is, but most people don't really know how to provide outstanding customer service. Customer service is much more than having a great attitude or being a people person. To prepare to provide excellent customer service, one must develop the skills to be successful.

In addition to developing employees' skills, organizations must assess what their current level of customer service is and determine if it appropriately meets their current customers' needs. Customers change all of the time, and the circumstances within which customers and organizations are required to operate are also changing. If customer policies were established a number of years ago, or if the customer base has changed, current procedures for operation may no longer be effective. Companies must develop strategies that meet today's customer's needs.

Employees must be empowered to make decisions to benefit their customers. They must have managers who carefully hired the right people for the job and employees who are adequately trained to anticipate the challenges that may arise daily. While customer service is more than having a great attitude, it does require having the right attitude. Some people become so involved in trying to provide excellent customer service that they lose sight of the little things that the customer would appreciate.

The use of technology and current information greatly facilitates the provision of excellent customer service. We live in an age of technology where a new and improved model is on the market almost before a new system is installed. Technology and information must work together to enhance customer service. Many up-to-date computer systems, e-mail, fax machines, printers, and messaging centers have remained unused because the information needed for their use was not developed and distributed to the appropriate customer service personnel. Customers use technology to enhance their own lives and they expect the businesses that they work with to use it also. Sometimes, having too much information or difficult-to-understand information is the challenge. Management must determine its relative importance in the total scheme of what the business is trying to accomplish. If we determine what our customer's concerns are, but we don't know how to include the customer's home address in our database effectively, we may conclude that we do not have the most important information that the customer has given us.

The challenge of providing excellent customer service never ends. Individuals must periodically examine their performance to ensure that they are continuing to practice the positive skills that make providing customer service enjoyable and efficient. It is easy to slip into old behaviors when we are busy or have additional stress in our lives.

Management must periodically measure customer satisfaction. Just because an organization thinks that its customers are pleased with what the organization is doing for them doesn't mean that this is true. Questions have to be asked of the customer concerning what is being done well and what could be improved. Customers have many concerns in their lives; just because they have not complained to us doesn't mean that they don't have complaints or suggestions. It may mean that we haven't gone to the trouble of asking.

One of the best ways to become a better customer service provider is to become a better customer. As we exercise our rights as customers, we become more sensitive to and aware of what it takes to become an excellent customer service provider. What bothers each of us probably bothers our customers. Exercise your rights as a customer. Write compliment and complaint letters to share your experiences and opinions. Fill out comment cards and answer truthfully when someone asks how your experience was. Don't expect more of others than you do of yourself. You may learn more from your opinions than the people you are sharing them with.

FIVE NEEDS OF EVERY CUSTOMER

Every customer comes into the customer situation with differing wants. While wants are frequently hard to identify and may occasionally be unrealistic, all customers have the following five basic needs:

1. *Service:* Customers expect the service they consider is appropriate for the level of purchase that they are making. A small, spontaneous purchase may have a smaller service need than a larger purchase that has been carefully planned and researched.
2. *Price:* The cost of everything we purchase is becoming more and more important. People and businesses want to use their financial resources as efficiently as possible. Many products previously con-

sidered unique offerings are now considered commodities. This means that while a consumer previously had to travel to the local hamburger restaurant to purchase a hamburger, now one can be acquired at many other locations. This makes the component of price even more important to the customer.

3. *Quality:* Americans are less likely today to think of their purchases as throwaway items. Customers want the products that they purchase to be durable and functional until the customer decides to replace them. This requirement of quality mandates that manufacturers and distributors produce products that live up to the customers' expectations of durability. Customers are much less likely to question price if they are doing business with a company that has a reputation for producing a high quality product.

4. *Action:* Customers need action when a problem or question arises. Many companies offer toll-free customer assistance telephone lines, flexible return policies, and customer carryout services in response to the need for action. Customers are human beings and like to think that they are an important priority and that when a need or question arises someone will be ready and waiting to help them.

5. *Appreciation:* Customers need to know that we appreciate their business. Customer service providers can convey this appreciation in many appropriate ways. Saying thank you to the customer through our words and actions is a good starting point. Preferred customer mailing lists, informational newsletters, special discounts, courtesy, and name recognition are good beginnings to showing our customers our appreciation. Additionally, letting them know that we are glad that they have chosen to do business with us conveys a positive message. A fast food restaurant has a sign in its drive-through lane that says, "We know that you could eat somewhere else; thank you for allowing us to serve you."

EXTERNAL AND INTERNAL CUSTOMERS

It is important to recognize the importance of both external and internal customers, because both contribute to the customer service of our organization. *External customers are the customers we do business with outside our organization.* External customers are those customers most commonly thought of when we consider whom we serve. They are the people with whom we interact and share our knowledge and positive attitude. External customers have the power to enhance our reputation and to bring us new business, but they are not the only customers that we serve.

Every day we interact with a special group of customers who frequently go unrecognized. These customers are our internal customers. *Our internal customers are the people we work with throughout our organization.* Our internal customers are important to our success in providing our external customers with what they need. If internal customers do not see the importance of completing work promptly and of treating others with respect, it becomes very difficult for the organization to provide outstanding customer service to our external customers. Internal customers were previously referred to as co-workers, but this title does not elicit the necessary respect deserved by the people within any organization who contribute to the overall success of the organization. Your customers may get a paycheck from the same company that you do.

The idea that all of us have customers does not appeal to those employees who want to think that since they do not interact with external customers they do not have a responsibility in the customer process. Our internal customers should be as important to us as our external customers.

By developing positive relationships with our internal customers we are showing them that we value their importance in the overall organization. We can apply a slightly modified version of the Golden Rule to our internal customers, "Do unto our internal customers as we would do unto ourselves." This rule suggests that as customer service providers we will strive to determine what our internal customers' needs and expectations are and place the same level of importance on their needs as on our own. We must stop and ask them what we can do to help make their jobs easier, and they should ask us the same thing. Working with our internal customers is not a form of manipulation, but instead a positive approach to being a part of a team. All the team members are working together to win, but not all are making the same type of contribution.

Management has an important role in creating an environment that recognizes the importance of internal customers. By providing opportunities for internal customers to experience the challenges of each other's responsibilities, an increased respect can develop. It also helps everyone involved to see the big picture. It is a natural human tendency to assume that someone else has an easier job and an easier life than we do. Obviously this is not necessarily the case. By beginning to understand your co-workers' challenges, you can work to minimize them. Systems may be redesigned, paperwork may be reduced, and a team approach may emerge.

By satisfying our internal customers, we are creating an excellent foundation on which to begin meeting our external customers' needs. Fewer apologies have to be made, work gets done more efficiently, and an overall positive atmosphere develops. If you cannot quite decide who your internal customers are, think of it this way, "Whose out-box do you work from and whose in-box do you feed into?" In addition to those people, who cleans the building, who does your typing, who maintains your security, who makes the sales, and who works on the computers? These are your internal customers. By being a part of a team with the goal of providing excellent customer service to all customers, a common vision of customer service may become a reality with real opportunities.

COST OF LOSING A CUSTOMER Because of the increased expectations of customers and the competitiveness of the marketplace, customer service providers are recognizing the high cost of losing customers. It takes little effort to lose customers. When service providers neglect their concerns, treat them with disrespect, and fail to follow through with results, customers will be tempted to make their exit.

When customers cease to do business with us and begin to do business with our competition, several unfortunate situations occur.

- We lose the **current dollars** that our business relationship created. This loss may seem insignificant to begin with, but over a period of time it can prove to be quite damaging.
- We lose the **jobs** that our client or clients provide. If business goes elsewhere, we do not need to employ the people who were working on the account or accounts. An advertising agency lost a major advertising account because of a lack of courtesy and follow-through on the agency's part. This loss of business resulted in the closing of the office, putting more than 50 people suddenly out of work.
- A third situation that may occur is the **loss of reputation.** Word travels fast in our information-based society. Our clients may share their experiences with their clients and friends. This loss may result in the immediate departure of other business or simply in a lack of trust among our current clients and any potential customers.
- A final challenge is the **loss of future business.** This is an intangible variable because it is difficult to assess the long-term effects of what might have happened in the future. Nevertheless, whether it is one dollar or a million dollars, its importance is worth recognizing.

SKILL BUILDING: "MY CUSTOMER"

Excellent customer service providers are continually assessing their own performance and the needs of their customers. The benefits of knowing our customers include enhanced service opportunities and an awareness of service weaknesses.

Individually, or in a small group, answer the following questions:

- **My customer** is satisfied when . . .

- **My customer** would like for me and my organization to improve our service by . . .

- I anticipate **my customer's** needs by . . .

- The most basic customer service action that I can take for **my customer** is . . .

- The greatest demands on me and my time are . . .

WRITING COMPLIMENT AND COMPLAINT LETTERS

One of the best ways to become a better customer service provider is to become a better customer. There are many ways of beginning the process necessary to become a better customer. An effective method for exercising your rights as a customer is to write compliment and complaint letters.

Many customer concerns are not effectively addressed when they occur and the customer continues to feel anger or frustration over the situation. By taking the initiative to express customer concerns or satisfaction a customer may feel closure in a given situation and has shared critical information with the organization.

When writing a complimentary letter it is important to include as many facts as possible. Unfortunately, most customers are much more interested in expressing their dissatisfaction than their satisfaction. By writing a complimentary letter you are giving an employee, department, or company a pat on the back that affirms for them that they are doing an effective job of meeting their customers' needs.

THE COMPLIMEN-TARY LETTER:

- Include your name, address, home and work telephone numbers, and account number, if appropriate.
- Make the letter brief and to the point. Share specific facts about the situation, including the name of the individual(s) who assisted you, the date of the interaction, and what pleased you.
- Type your letter if possible, it will look more professional and will be easier to read.
- Always keep a copy of any correspondence that you send. You may want it for future reference or to use as a sample for another complimentary letter in the future.

As with a complimentary letter, when writing a complaint letter it is important to include specific facts. Complaint letters should be to the point and unemotional. Complaint letters provide the writer with the opportunity to express concerns, to document grievances, and to request specific or non-specific resolutions to the situation.

THE COMPLAINT LETTER

- Include your name, address, home and work telephone numbers, and account number, if appropriate.
- Make your letter brief and to the point. Detail specific facts about the situation. Include the date and place of the purchase, and information about the product or service.
- State exactly how you would like to see the situation resolved and when you expect to see the resolution in effect.

- Type your letter if possible and include copies of all pertinent documents. Do not send originals, retain them along with a copy of your correspondence for future reference.
- The following sample complaint letter provides a guide to writing an effective complaint letter.

SAMPLE COMPLAINT LETTER

(Your address)
(Your city, state, ZIP code)
(Date)

(Name of contact person)
(Title)
(Company name)
(Street address)
(City, state, ZIP code)

Dear (contact person):

On (date), I bought (or had repaired) a (name of product with serial or model number or service performed). I made this purchase at (location, date and other important details of the transaction).

Unfortunately, your product (or service) had not performed well (or the service was inadequate) because (state the problem).

Therefore, to resolve the problem, I would appreciate you (state the specific action you want). Enclosed are copies (copies—not originals) of my records (receipts, guarantees, warranties, canceled checks, contracts, model and serial numbers, and any other documents).

I look forward to your reply and a resolution to my problem, and will wait (set time limit) before seeking third party assistance. Please contact me at the above address or by phone at the numbers shown below.

Sincerely,

(Your name)
(Office and home phone numbers with area code)
(Your account number)

Enclosures
Source: Southwestern Bell Telephone Book 1992–1993

CHALLENGE OBJECTIVES

1. To demonstrate the ability to express both positive and negative customer service experiences in print.
2. To explore the possibility of a corporate response to written communication.
3. To refine individual business communication skills.

CHALLENGE

Compose two letters explaining two separate customer service experiences that you or someone close to you has had. One letter should explain a positive experience and should show appreciation for those who offered the positive treatment. The second letter should express your dissatisfaction over a poor customer service experience. Try to include as many details as you can, including specific names, dates, etc. You may wish to ask for some type of follow-up if you feel that it would be appropriate in the situation. You are the judge of whether the situation is worthy of your correspondence.

PRESENTATION

All professional business correspondence should be typed on a computer, word processor, or typewriter. Follow the guidelines for writing a compliment/complaint letter. Always remember to include your full name and address so that the business will know who to send a response to. Be specific when describing what you would like to see happen in response to your letter. Always keep a copy of anything that you mail. You will have it to refer to in the future and can use it as an example when writing your next compliment/complaint letter. Most important, mail your letters! Record on your calendar when the letters were sent and watch the mail for a reply. Happy writing!

Helpful hint: Many word processing programs have "letter wizards" to assist you in writing professional letters. If you have limited experience with writing business letters, you may want to try one.

1. What is the definition of customer service?
2. List five examples of customer service.
3. What are the five needs that every customer has?
4. Explain why it is necessary for customer service providers to maintain positive relationships with both internal and external customers.
5. How is technology enhancing the provision of excellent customer service?
6. Relate customers' expectations about price to their expectations of service.
7. Is the loss of current dollars the only concern when a customer is lost?
8. List ways that you can become a better customer.
9. Write your own philosophy and definition of customer service.
10. Define contentment.

THE CHALLENGES OF CUSTOMER SERVICE

- **ELEMENTS OF SUCCESS**
- **BARRIERS TO EXCELLENT CUSTOMER SERVICE**
- **POWER OF PERCEPTIONS**
- **UNDERSTANDING OF EXPECTATIONS**
- **LEVELS OF EXPECTATIONS**
- **SCOPE OF INFLUENCE**
- **REPUTATION MANAGEMENT**
- **TECHNIQUES FOR EXCEEDING CUSTOMERS' EXPECTATIONS**
- **KEYS TO CREDIBILITY**
- **IMPORTANCE OF VALUES**
- **ETHICS IN CUSTOMER SERVICE**
- **CURRENT STATUS OF CUSTOMER SERVICE**
- **NEW TRENDS IN CUSTOMER SERVICE**
- **SKILL BUILDING: UNDERSTANDING EXPECTATIONS**
- **OPPORTUNITIES FOR CRITICAL THINKING**

REMEMBER THIS
A reputation once broken may possibly be repaired, but the world will always keep its eyes on the spot where the crack was.

JOSEPH HALL

ELEMENTS OF SUCCESS

Customer service is such a valuable concept that it seems it would be simple to provide it. Unfortunately, this is not necessarily the case. After assessing their own strengths and weaknesses, customer service providers must begin to understand the customers that they are serving. After doing this, they may begin to be prepared to provide those customers with excellent customer service. By becoming familiar with the various barriers to customer service, recognizing the power of perceptions, understanding expectations, and maintaining their own credibility and sense of values, customer service providers are equipping themselves to fully serve their customers.

BARRIERS TO EXCELLENT CUSTOMER SERVICE

Numerous obstacles stand in the way of delivering excellent customer service. Some of the common barriers include management philosophy; making it difficult for customers with a problem to contact a company or the person who can really help; unreliable equipment; restrictive company policies; difficult-to-understand warranties or owner's manuals; out-of-date procedures; or a lack of understanding of the value of service. These barriers are, in most cases, beyond the control of the customer service provider and, unfortunately, a common part of doing the job.

Some barriers to excellent customer service are within the control of the customer service provider. These are challenges that can be overcome through diligent effort, allowing the customer service provider to do the best possible job. Some of these barriers that can be overcome are:

1. Laziness
2. Poor communication skills
3. Poor time management
4. Attitude
5. Moodiness
6. Lack of adequate training
7. Inability to handle stress
8. Insufficient authority
9. Serving customers "on autopilot"
10. Inadequate staffing

Customer service providers must perform periodic self-evaluations to assess their effectiveness and to identify areas in need of improvement. When that assessment is made, individuals must take the initiative to change and then monitor themselves so that they don't slip into their old habits.

POWER OF PERCEPTIONS

Any time that we interact with others we must be aware of their perceptions of situations, experiences, and people. *A perception is the way that we see something based on our experience.* Everyone's perception of a situation will be, at least slightly, different. The question persists, "Is the glass half full or is it half empty?"

Perceptions are frequently developed over a period of time and reflect the ways that we have been treated, our values, priorities, prejudices, and sensitivity to others. Two people could share the same experience and then describe it differently. Unfortunately, perceptions are not necessarily based on rational ideas and may be influenced by momentary frustration and anger. Because perceptions are so full of mystery, it is important for the customer service provider to anticipate customer resistance based on the customers' prior interactions and always to work at providing customers with excellent service, so that their most current perception is a positive one. Customers may not remember every detail of an experience, but they will retain an overall feeling about it. That "feeling," in combination with other experiences, will create their perception of your company and you.

Whenever possible, try to deal with your customers as individual human beings. Respect their time, circumstances, and priorities. Always convey to customers that you appreciate the time it takes them to do business with your company. Ask the customers if there is anything else that you can do for them. Periodically, ask the customers how you are doing. The feedback that they give you will provide insights as to how they perceive your organization. Remember that you may not be able to erase customers' negative perceptions that are based on their prior interactions. What you can do is to show them, through your actions, that their perception is not accurate.

UNDER- STANDING OF EXPECTATIONS

Every customer walks into a known or unknown situation with a set of expectations as to what will transpire. *Expectations are our personal vision of the result that will come from our experience.* Expectations may be positive or negative. How many times have you practiced your response to an anticipated objection only to find out that you didn't have to use it? Expectations are usually based, at least partially, on our perceptions. If your last experience with a company was negative, you may approach a new situation with the expectation that you will again be dissatisfied. Because of this, you may approach the interaction "armed and ready" for battle.

Sometimes companies or individuals wrongly assume that they cannot live up to their customers' expectations. This assumption is frequently due to a misconception of what the customers expect.

At an educational institution, school representatives and students were informally surveyed to determine what expectations the students had of the institution. The results showed a broad disparity between what the students expected and what the school representatives thought the students expected. The representatives of the school ranked the students' top five expectations of the school. They were as follows:

1. Grades with no effort
2. Extra assistance with enrollment
3. Short classes
4. No reading assignments
5. More parking

The students ranked their own expectations this way:

1. Positive environment that encouraged learning
2. Transferable classes
3. Instructors who cared and knew the students' names
4. Safety in the parking lot and building
5. More parking

It is easy to identify the differences between the two lists. It would be incorrect to assume that all students shared the surveyed students' expectations. It would also be incorrect to assume that there weren't some students who did have the expectations that the school representatives perceived that they had.

What is important to learn from this comparison is that what our customers expect is frequently much easier and less costly to provide than we may think. What the students expected cost relatively little or nothing to provide, but since the school didn't know what the students' expectations were, the expectations were not being consistently realized.

LEVELS OF EXPECTATIONS

Customer service providers must recognize that customers have different levels of expectations. Expectations can be divided into two distinct categories: primary expectations and secondary expectations.

Primary expectations are the customers' most basic requirements of an interaction. When dining at a restaurant, our primary expectations are to satisfy our hunger, to let someone else do the cooking, and to pay a reasonable price.

Secondary expectations are expectations based on our previous experiences and represent enhancements to our primary expectations. When dining at a restaurant, our secondary expectations include good service, courtesy, and good, tasty food.

A customer's expectations are constantly changing, and each customer will have his or her own unique set of expectations. While this is a challenging reality, it can provide a unique opportunity for us to consistently strive to be what the customers want us to be.

SCOPE OF INFLUENCE

It is important for businesses to recognize the influence that their customers have on other customers and potential customers. This influence is called scope of influence. *Scope of influence is our ability to influence others based on our perceptions or experiences.* Each person's "scope" is different. The average number of people that our opinions influence is, on average, between 7 and 15 people. This range may be understated. Some people have a larger scope because they interact with a larger number of people or because they have outgoing, open personalities.

Scope of influence plays no favorites and is usually not objective. Thus, it is extremely important to do all we can to make our customers happy and to keep their business. Studies have shown that it costs about five times as much to attract new customers as it costs to keep our current customers. Research has also shown that customers are more likely to share a negative experience with their superiors. These superiors are frequently the people with more decision-making power, income, and influence. Unfortunately, customers are likely to share positive experiences with the people closest to them and with no one else.

Marketing professionals have long recognized the power of word-of-mouth advertising. This is basically what scope of influence is. We must ask, remind, and entice our customers to share their positive experiences with others. By doing so, we are showing our current customers how much we appreciate them, and we are also creating an opportunity for new customers to come to us expecting a positive experience. A happy customer can attract new customers at virtually no cost.

REPUTATION MANAGEMENT

One way that some companies to differentiate themselves from the competition is through reputation management. *Reputation management is the process of identifying how a company is perceived and establishing an action plan to correct, maintain, or enhance the company's reputation.* As more and more products and services become commodities, customers may be more attracted to a company because of its reputation than any other single factor. Reputation management moves away from how a company would like to be perceived and identifies and responds to how they really are perceived. A good reputation is cultivated over time through a company, department, or individual's performance, good or bad, in a variety of situations.

A company seeking to begin to manage its reputation must survey its customers and the community at large to assess what its reputation really is. A company's reputation is different from its image. A company could have a positive image, but not a positive reputation. A company could be recognized as being a positive and likeable member of the community, but when it comes time to do business with them, customers consistently decide to take their business elsewhere.

According to the marketing research firm Yankelovich & Partners, a company with a good reputation:

- Is very responsive to customers.
- Is a company you can trust.
- Delivers on its promises to customers.
- Provides excellent value to customers.
- Has excellent communications.
- Is ethical and honest.
- Conducts business in a human/caring way.
- Has excellent top management.
- Is able to adapt to changes in its industry.
- Is a good citizen.

- Is a progressive company.
- Is cooperative.
- Has a record of strong financial performance.
- Treats employees with respect.
- Is a technological leader in its industry.
- Is committed to the environment.
- Complies with state/federal regulations.
- Is successful in diversifying operations. (*Industry Week,* February 3, 1997, pp. 13–16).

By effectively managing its reputation, a company can maintain an informed and realistic understanding of how customers and the community perceive it, which can help it to anticipate and plan for challenges in the future.

TECHNIQUES FOR EXCEEDING CUSTOMERS' EXPECTATIONS

To begin the process of attempting to exceed our customers' expectations, try the following:

1. **Become familiar with your customers.** Get to know who they are and why they do business with you. Find out their likes and dislikes.
2. **Ask your customers what their expectations are.** Find out what they see as the benefit of doing business with you. What would they like for you to do that you aren't already doing?
3. **Tell your customers what they can expect.** Convey to your customers your commitment to them.
4. **Live up to their expectations.** Follow through by accomplishing what you have said that you would do.
5. **Maintain consistency.** Don't promise what you cannot deliver, but always deliver a consistent service. Customers like to know that they will have the same positive experience every time that they interact with you.

One important key to exceeding your customers' expectations is to remember that expectations are always changing. What was previously in excess of our customers' expectations may suddenly be no different from what all of our competition is doing. If we fail to stay current with our competition, we may fail to live up to our customers' current expectations.

The American auto industry was for many years the world standard for excellence in automobiles. With many loyal customers, its position in the marketplace seemed secure. It had set the standard of excellence. At the same time the foreign automakers were observing what customers seemed to like and to dislike. The Americans paid little attention to this potential competition; after all, they had set the standard. Suddenly, seemingly out of nowhere, a new group of competitors had entered the marketplace. These new competitors knew what customers liked and disliked about American cars. The American auto industry was shocked; how could their customers turn their backs on them and purchase automobiles from a non-American manufacturer?

Unfortunately, what the American automakers failed to remember is that once a standard is set, it represents an opportunity for the competition to attempt to surpass it. No industry has ever continued to maintain a loyal customer base without continuously recognizing what the competition is doing and continuing to meet the customers' ever-changing needs and wants. Fortunately, the American auto industry has recognized what the competition is doing and is regaining many of the customers that they had previously lost.

KEYS TO CREDIBILITY In all aspects of our lives we are confronted with the challenge of being believable to those around us. How believable we are, in combination with how reliable we are, translates into how credible we are to others. *Credibility is made up of the combination of our current knowledge, reputation, and professionalism.* Credibility encourages trust. If we are to work successfully with our customers, they must trust us. Our personal credibility can be the one characteristic that determines our success as people and as customer service providers.

Try these tips for cultivating credibility:

1. **Practice consistency.** Approach similar situations in the same manner, always striving for fairness. Demonstrate your emotional stability. Be positive, professional, and warm at all times.
2. **Keep your word.** Follow through with the commitments you make. Any call you receive expresses the implication that you will respond with answers. People will not have faith in you if you break your promises.
3. **Develop your expertise.** Become very knowledgeable about your products, your company, and the overall industry. Strive for continuous improvement.
4. **Become a teammate with your co-workers.** By working successfully with others, you show that you have common goals and can benefit from each individual's specific skills.
5. **Show your dedication to customers.** Tell customers what you will do for them, take every request seriously, and follow up.
6. **Treat all of your customers and co-workers with the same high level of respect.** By showing that you respect others, you create an environment that allows others to respect you. Be sensitive to your effect on customers.
7. **Apologize if you are wrong.** Your honesty will impress customers and they will respect you for who you are, not who you pretend to be.
8. **Remember that credibility is much harder to regain than it is to keep.**

IMPORTANCE OF VALUES

For excellent customer service to exist, the successful joining of corporate values and employee values has to occur. *Values are a combination of our beliefs, perceptions, and ideas as to the appropriate response to a situation.* Both individuals and companies have their own specific sets of values. Companies must effectively communicate to their employees what the company's values are. Stated corporate values are most commonly conveyed to employees through written information in employee manuals or policy statements. Real corporate values can also be conveyed through the actions of the management in an organization. Employees must recognize their own values and beliefs and attempt to identify organizations that have similar priorities.

Individual values are very personal. No other person has experienced exactly the circumstances that have allowed you to develop the values that you possess. In the customer service industry, some organizations have a very distinct set of dos and don'ts. Other organizations may be more vague in expressing to employees what the corporate priorities are. In either instance the customer service providers must recognize that they are both representatives of their company and individuals. The behaviors and philosophies illustrate the persons they are.

ETHICS IN CUSTOMER SERVICE

Most individuals are faced periodically with situations that they may find to be ethically challenging. What exactly are ethics and why do they matter in our professional and personal lives? *Ethics are a set of principles that govern the conduct of an individual or group.* Sometimes ethical decisions are easy to recognize and are perceived as popular choices of behavior by the people around us. At other times the spectrum of potential choices falls into gray areas in which the "right" or "wrong" course of action is difficult or nearly impossible to identify. The challenge of ethical decision making becomes even harder when it is not just an individual's personal judgement that is involved, but also carrying out the instructions of a supervisor, the request of a customer, the policy of the organization, or some other situation in which a threat, real or perceived, is involved.

There are really no shortcuts when it comes to telling the truth and determining an appropriate course of action. Individuals in business must be seen by those around them as honest, or they will not succeed for long. The bottom line in decision making is that individuals must face the consequences of the decisions they make—good or bad. A quick checklist to go through when faced with an ethically challenging situation is to ask yourself the following questions.

Ethics checklist:

• Is it legal?
• Is it fair?

- How do I feel about it?
- Would the court of public opinion find my behavior incorrect?
- Am I fearful of what those I trust would say about my actions?

The above questions can be quite revealing when attempting to choose an ethical course of action. This is not to suggest that ethically challenging situations are easily resolved, but by analyzing a situation the appropriate decision may be easier to identify. One final consideration regarding ethical behavior is that it is not always popular to "do the right thing," but maintaining individual integrity and an organization's reputation will allow all involved to know that they examined all possibilities and chose the most appropriate course of action.

CURRENT STATUS OF CUSTOMER SERVICE

Today everyone is talking about how important customer service is, but they are, for the most part, doing very little to improve it. This can be attributed to several causes.

1. It is frequently difficult to measure the financial benefits of customer service. It may be challenging to convince some financial managers of the long-term payoffs.
2. Customers have high expectations of what they hope to gain from the people with whom they do business, but frequently customer service providers don't know what those expectations are.
3. Customers have grown accustomed to expecting improved levels of customer service and considerable latitude when it comes to receiving customer service, but the resulting cost may be prohibitive for many businesses. Frequently, the customers who take advantage of customer-friendly policies are abusing the opportunity and represent minimal percentages of the overall business. Businesses now have to manage customers' expectations about what is appropriate and realistic.
4. Technology provides the opportunity for faster responses to customer questions, but it has also created the requirement that customer service providers have additional training to become proficient in using new systems.
5. Customer service is an opportunity that no professional can afford to ignore. It is frequently the distinguishing difference between two or more companies that offer the same product or service.

NEW TRENDS IN CUSTOMER SERVICE

Several new trends are emerging in the customer service industry. These trends reflect the ways in which customers approach a business interaction and the ways that businesses are preparing to respond to them. The trends include accessibility for the customer, immediacy of response, feedback from customer to customer service provider, outsourcing of all or part of customer service functions, and non-traditional examples of customer service.

Customers today have more access to information about their account status, billing, delivery, and product availability than ever before. This accessibility has, in many cases, reduced the questions that customer service providers must respond to, leaving them to respond to more unique requests. An example of this accessibility is found in customer information hot lines that can be reached from a touch-tone telephone using personal identification numbers; a second example is computer software that tracks where a shipment is, whether the shipment has been received, and by whom. Customers appreciate the control that this accessibility allows them, and it reduces the number of routine questions that customer service providers must answer. It is also a wonderful illustration of technology at work.

The immediacy of response is another trend in customer service. Again, because of technology, customers can have questions or problems resolved almost immediately. Customer service providers are also more fully empowered to make decisions in response to customer inquiries that previously would have been taken to a higher level supervisor.

Feedback is important to all businesses and can provide opportunities for growth in the customer service department. Customer suggestions are now frequently requested and encouraged. Independent research departments or survey companies may contact customers. Customer service providers are also beginning to keep logs of customer suggestions and requests so that improvements can be efficiently made. Customers appreciate the chance to share their ideas and to see changes being made.

As businesses seek new strategies to improve performance, save money, and effectively address increasingly technical requests, outsourcing may be an effective alternative. Competition has forced many industries to begin outsourcing such functions as payroll, data processing, billing, maintenance, marketing, accounts receivable, and many more. The specialized customer service needs of many businesses are also being outsourced. Outsourcing can provide cost savings in rent, benefits, equipment, and short-term employee expense; in addition, it can allow organizations of all sizes to better serve their customers. Most organizations receive customer questions, complaints, and comments via 800 numbers and e-mail. While this allows closer interaction with customers, it also has increased the expected response time. The necessary equipment to receive and respond to these contacts is costly, the added cost of hiring and training effective customer service representatives may mean that some organizations cannot afford to provide this service to their customers. Hiring a carefully chosen outside company to handle specialized technical questions, customer concerns, and product inquiries can increase customer response time and share the cost of providing the service among participating companies. The most positive potential benefit is the goal of increasing customer retention—keeping current customers actively involved in doing business because their needs are met and they are never tempted to look elsewhere to seek better service.

Customer service is an important part of the overall marketing strategy. This has encouraged the development of some non-traditional approaches to customer service. One example is offering customers informational newsletters. Informational newsletters mailed periodically or handed out are nonthreatening to customers because they share information, new product or service offerings, new systems, or service hours; they also remind the customer that the company is available and ready to serve them again. Newsletters can have the luxury of being seen by customers as informational pieces that aren't trying to sell something. They are really selling the company, but the approach is subtler; therefore, it is less threatening.

SKILL BUILDING: *UNDERSTANDING EXPECTATIONS*

All customers have their own unique set of expectations. Expectations may be positive or negative. Organizations must periodically attempt to determine what their customers expect from their customer experience.

Individually, or in small groups of three or four, list the top four expectations that customers would have of the following organizations.

- Prestige hotel
- Electric company
- Nationally recognized fast food chain
- Auto service department or garage
- Car rental company
- Local community college
- Credit card company
- Your own organization or department

After determining the top four expectations of each of the above organizations, rank the expectations from easiest to most difficult to provide. Attempt to draw conclusions from your rankings.

A common observation when customer expectations are evaluated is that many of the expectations that customers have are easy and inexpensive to provide. By attempting to understand customers' expectations, organizations have the unique opportunity to consistently strive to be what customers want them to be.

OPPORTUNITIES FOR CRITICAL THINKING

1. Why is it important to convey credibility to your customer?
2. Explain the five techniques for exceeding customers' expectations.
3. Why are so many people talking about customer service and yet doing so little to improve its quality?
4. Why should we consider our customer's perceptions?
5. What are some common barriers to customer service?
6. How relevant is the reality that some customers may perceive your service inaccurately?
7. How do primary expectations differ from secondary expectations?
8. Describe an example of a situation where scope of influence hurt or helped your business.
9. What are some techniques for conveying credibility to others?
10. What role do values play in an individual's approach to providing customer service?

PROBLEM SOLVING

REMEMBER THIS

*We are continually faced by great opportunities
brilliantly disguised as insoluble problems.*

UNKNOWN

ROLE OF PROBLEM SOLVING IN CUSTOMER SERVICE

Most individuals encounter frequently the need to solve problems. In many instances problems are challenges that we would prefer to avoid, but in most cases, this is not a possibility. One of the important activities in which customer service providers participate is helping to solve customers' problems. *Problem solving is an active resolution to a challenging situation.*

Many individuals dread problem solving. It can add considerable stress to an otherwise peaceful work environment. One of the main reasons that problem solving is perceived as unpleasant is that the average business professional has not worked to develop the skills necessary to accomplish it effectively and efficiently. The only training some people have is the memory of the way they observed their own families dealing with problems as they were growing up. This example is frequently not transferable to a business environment. Most individuals in an organization are aware of the repercussions that can result from an incorrect resolution to problems. Because of this they may be reluctant to take the responsibility which accompanies problem solving.

To actively confront the challenge of problem solving, organizations must prepare employees with training in possible approaches to problem solving. They must create a safe environment, which encourages employees to develop solutions that are positive for both the customer and the company.

Problem solving and decision making are individualized processes. Every individual may have his or her own method of determining an appropriate course of action. What is important is the end result, not the process of determining the solution. As long as the solution is timely, the process is less important.

One significant challenge to problem solving when interacting with customers is the speed with which decisions must be made. A customer may call with a question or problem and the customer service provider may only have a few seconds to a few minutes to provide the customer with an answer. Unfortunately, this does not allow for much time to examine possible solutions. Customer service providers must become highly proficient in listening to a customer's explanation of a situation or problem, in asking pertinent questions to clarify the information, and in providing the customer with an appropriate solution. The solution must be one that they are willing to share regardless of the possible repercussions.

Customer service providers can effectively equip themselves to make decisions and to solve problems by learning problem-solving strategies, developing negotiation skills, learning how to deal effectively with conflict, and recognizing the importance of follow-up.

CREATIVITY AND PROBLEM SOLVING

When individuals solving problems incorporate creativity into the process of problem solving, positive challenges result. Creative problem solving suggests that through an open approach to finding solutions, an appropriate and innovative result may be discovered. Creative problem solving requires that employees work in a culture that allows new ideas to flow freely and to be realistically considered. When the same problems consistently arise and are resolved in the same established manner, the opportunity for a new and more creative resolution may exist.

Customers appreciate creativity. Creativity requires effort and commitment to creating a new idea or solution. The individuals in an organization who are the closest to the customers are those who interact with them on an ongoing basis. In many organizations these individuals are the customer service providers. By offering suggestions to customers and to management about innovative and new ways of solving challenges, customer service providers can share their creativity with others.

PROBLEMS AS OPPORTUNITIES Criticism is an opportunity to obtain information. When customers express problems or frustrations, it is easy to become defensive. A productive method of response to criticism is to consider the criticism as productive input to the creation of a problem-solving environment. A customer complaint is really a request for action.

Customers frequently have ideas about how a problem might be avoided in the future. By offering them the opportunity to share their ideas, we allow them to participate in the process of improving a situation or system with which they are disappointed. This allows a team effort that creates unity between provider and customer.

CONFRONTING CONFLICT Conflict is a reality of most approaches to problem solving. Problem solving and decision making involve the consideration of possible alternatives and the selection of the alternative that is viewed by the decision maker as being the most appropriate. This does not mean that all the parties involved will agree that the chosen course of action is the best. This may create conflict in some situations. *Conflict is a hostile encounter that occurs as a result of opposing needs, wishes, or ideas.* Conflict can occur among even the most cohesive employee team or with our most faithful customers. When faced with conflict and disagreement it is important to proceed with caution! Many words have been spoken in anger, creating damage that was difficult to correct. The goal in any problem-solving environment, even when anger is present, is not to win an argument, but to resolve a conflict.

When encountering conflict, remember the following suggestions:

1. Listen to the other viewpoints that are being presented.
2. Do not bring up old problems from the past or assign blame.
3. Use tact as you respond to others.
4. Do not repress your own anger, instead use it productively. Take advantage of the opportunity to share other related concerns in a positive manner.
5. Focus on finding the best solution to the conflict.

PROBLEM- Numerous approaches may be taken when attempting to solve problems.
SOLVING After determining that a problem exists, it is helpful to respond to the fol-
PROCESS lowing guidelines. The guidelines are represented as they occur on the fol-
lowing problem-solving model (Figure 3-1).

1. **Identify the problem.** Attempt to recognize and understand what
   the real problem is. Sometimes the true problem will be difficult to
   identify because of other variables that are more recognizable, but
   that do not represent the problem that requires solving.
2. **Understand the problem's unique characteristics and the possible
   outcomes.** The problems that must be solved by customer service
   providers frequently have unique characteristics. These unique
   characteristics may have no bearing on the solution that is to be determined, but they must be considered while a solution is being
   developed.
3. **Define the requirements of a possible solution considering the
   company policies currently in place.** Frequent requests may have
   resulted in policies being developed to promote consistency in the
   way that they were handled. The requirements of the solution must
   be determined and the policies considered. Policies that are flexible
   should be considered as opportunities.
4. **Identify possible solutions.** Frequently, the success of a problem's
   solution has to do with the generation of more than one possible solution and the selection of the best solution. As possible solutions are
   considered, they should reflect an array of alternatives and the individuals who will be affected.
5. **Select the best solution.** Selecting the best solution may be the most
   challenging aspect of the problem-solving process. The positive and
   negative results must be considered from both the company's and
   the customer's perspective.
6. **Implement the solution, informing the customer of the details
   and of how they will be affected.** Putting the solution into place is
   an integral part of the problem-solving process. Until the solution is
   implemented, from the customer's viewpoint nothing has been
   done. The most creative solution has little value if it is not put into
   action. Communication is important at this time. Everyone who
   will be affected by the solution must be informed of its implementation and any responsibility that they may have in contributing to
   its success.
7. **Observe and evaluate the solution's impact.** After a solution has
   been implemented, it should be observed and evaluated to determine whether it was successful. Observation can occur on an ongoing basis, but a formal evaluation should be scheduled to take place
   at a designated time.

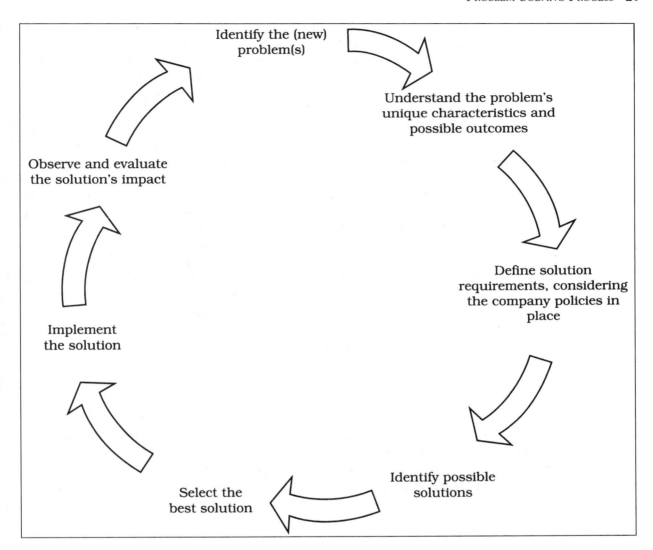

Figure 3-1
The Problem-
Solving Model

The problem-solving process should follow the guidelines included in the model. If steps are skipped or overlooked, serious errors may occur in the solutions. For example, a courier company's delivery people did not have time to read their mail. Important information was not getting to the appropriate people because of the problem. A meeting was called by various members of management to attempt to solve the situation. After a brief explanation of the problem was given, members of the group began sharing their solutions. Some of the ideas were to begin forwarding all the employees' mail to their homes so that they would have more time to read it, to purchase laptop computers for all of the couriers so that they could receive electronic mail, and to reprimand the employees for their oversight. The most popular solution from those mentioned was to forward the mail to the employees' homes. The management team began discussing how to print address labels and what type of envelopes to use.

One of the managers believed that the solution of mailing materials twice was premature. She shared with the other managers that although mailing material twice would guarantee that the employees received their mail, it would not guarantee that they would actually read it. She suggested that it might be appropriate to find out why the employees were not reading their mail. This provoked a more focused approach to problem solving. At this time the group began to follow the problem-solving process as they attempted to understand and to solve the mail problem.

Upon further analysis it was determined that one of the major problems was that employees received as many as 100 documents a day. Every memorandum that was circulated in the company was sent to every employee, even when it did not directly affect him or her. Since a courier's main function is to deliver materials, it was difficult for them to read mail and to drive, especially when much of the mail was useless to them. The management team began to see that the problem was not just the fault of the employees, but was also a shared responsibility of the management team. A solution to the problem was developed to meet the needs of all involved. If the manager had not voiced her concerns about the original solution to what was perceived as the problem, the company would have been spending a lot of money on postage to send mail to employees who did not need to read it.

PROBLEM-SOLVING STRATEGIES

When approaching the challenge of determining a solution for a problem, individual strategies or a combination of strategies may be used. To effectively determine solutions it may be helpful to follow methods that have been proven to create positive results. The two common strategies of problem solving are brainstorming and diagramming.

BRAINSTORMING

Brainstorming is a problem-solving strategy that can be used by groups of two or more. The premise behind brainstorming is that the more ideas that are shared in an open and accepting environment, the more creativity will result. As ideas are shared, other ideas may develop. A group approach to problem solving like brainstorming can create a unique and creative opportunity to generate solutions.

To begin a brainstorming exercise, a group should gather willing to share ideas. A specific problem should be identified. One individual should be designated as the recorder. He or she should be responsible for recording the ideas shared.

The next step in a successful brainstorming activity is for someone to share the first idea. Other ideas should follow. The more ideas generated, the better. Ideas frequently stimulate other ideas. It is mandatory for the leaders who are facilitating the exercise to create an accepting environment in which the participants can operate. If individuals are afraid that their ideas will be rejected or that they will be ridiculed for their suggestions, they will be less likely to participate.

When several ideas have been generated, a master list should be prepared. The master list can be displayed immediately on a flip chart or chalkboard. The master list can also be compiled and distributed to group members for later discussion. The members can review the ideas and make additions. A second meeting should be held to make recommendations for the most appropriate problem-solving solution. By allowing group members to review all of the ideas that were shared, it should be easier to determine which ideas are possible solutions to the problem. The chosen solutions can begin to be implemented, and, hopefully, the problem is on its way to being resolved.

DIAGRAMMING

Diagramming is a strategy for problem solving that provides a visual representation of the problem and the facts related to it. Visual representations are easy to work with because they allow a visual examination as well as an oral discussion. There are four main methods of diagramming problems in search of appropriate solutions. The three methods are: Pro/con sheets, flow-charts, organizational charts, and mind mapping.

1. **Pro/con sheets:** A simple approach to diagramming a problem is the use of pro/con sheets (Figure 3-2). Pro/con sheets are best when used to choose a specific course of action as the resolution to a problem. To create a pro/con sheet, write the problem and the possible solution on a sheet of paper. Then draw a line down the center and write the word *pro* on one side of the line and *con* on the other side of the line. The next step is to write all of the positive reasons that the solution would work on the pro side of the line. All of the reasons why the solution would not be appropriate should be listed on the con side. When all of the reasons for and against a possible solution are listed, it can be determined whether the solution is appropriate or not. Pro/con sheets are simple, but this is one reason they can work well in choosing a solution.

2. **Flow-charts:** When using flow-charts in the problem-solving process, it is helpful to diagram what the process or flow of a problem is (Figure 3-3). Sometimes just listing how a situation is processed and who must be involved is enough to identify the reason for a problem. To create a flow-chart, include in a box on the top of a sheet of paper the point where a process begins. An example might be: Who has to authorize an extension on a payment for a customer? If the beginning of the process starts with the customer

Figure 3-2
Pro/Con Sheet

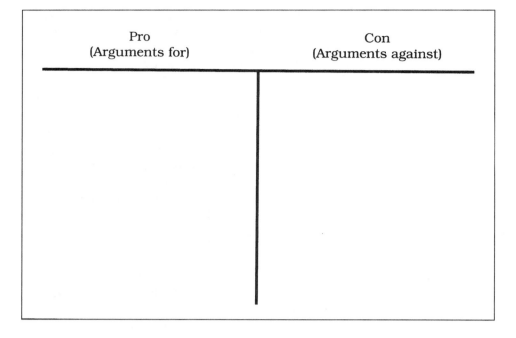

Pro (Arguments for)	Con (Arguments against)

making the request, this would go in the first box. The person whom the customer calls would go in the second box. The third box would be for the person whom the employee must ask to gain approval for the payment extension. If the customer's records must be retrieved from another department, this would go in the next box. The process would go on from there.

Diagramming the current system for responding to the customer's request makes it easier to understand why the process took longer than appropriate. Flow-charts are helpful in identifying unnecessary steps in a process. They can also assist in identifying who would be affected by a change in the method of processing information.

3. **Organizational charts:** A commonly used method of illustrating the hierarchy of a company is with organizational charts (Figure 3-4). An organizational chart is a diagram of who reports to whom within an organization or department. While organizational charts will not assist in solving specific problems, they can provide a visual illustration of areas of employee overload and can reveal possible snags in the success of a system. If someone is required to give authorization to a new project, but is involved in managing another area of the business, he or she may not have the knowledge to make the most effective decisions. In addition, if the person is not involved in the same part of the process, he or she may not be aware of the day-to-day challenges encountered by employees.

**Figure 3-3
Flowchart**

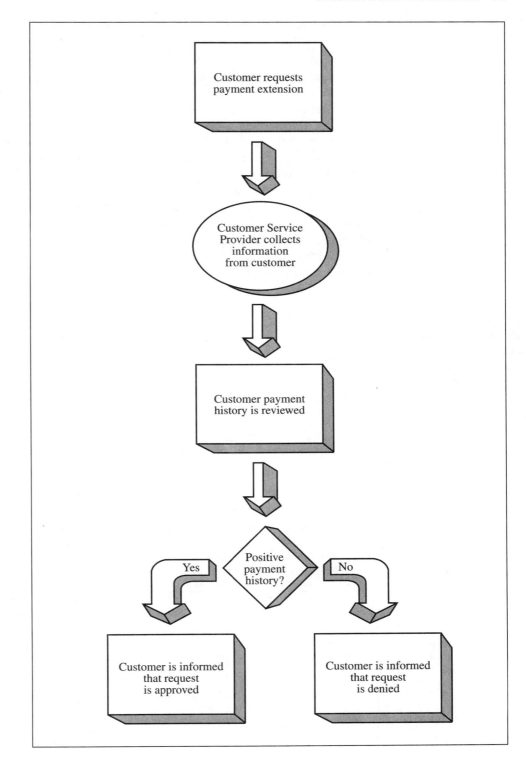

4. Mind mapping: An extremely creative approach to diagramming a problem is mind mapping (Figure 3-5). The concept of mind mapping was developed in the 1970s and is still popular today. Mind mapping involves the practical aspects of traditional problem solving while incorporating the opportunity to freely approach new ways of thinking.

To begin a mind-map, place the problem or decision in an oval in the center of a large piece of paper. The center placement symbolizes that the problem or decision is the core of your map. After creating the center, place lines coming out of the center going in different directions. On the lines write important words or phrases that pertain to finding a solution to the challenge. Add additional branches coming off the important words or phrases. These branches should list ideas or thoughts that relate to the solution of the problem. Try to come up with ideas as quickly as possible. The more outlandish and creative the ideas are the better. Quality is not impor-

Figure 3-4
Organizational
Chart

(*Trinity Software, Ltd.*
January 19, 1995)

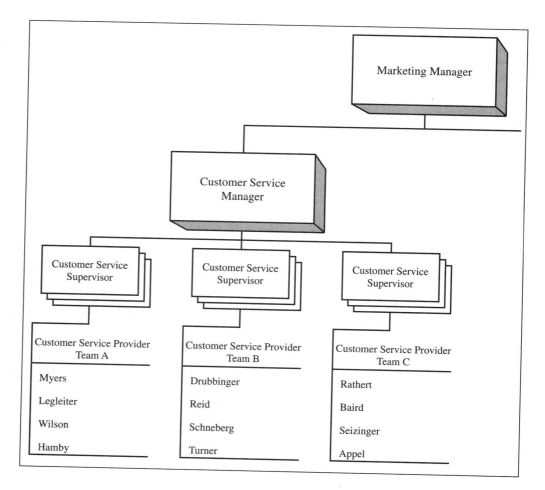

Customer Service Provider Team A	Customer Service Provider Team B	Customer Service Provider Team C
Myers	Drubbinger	Rathert
Legleiter	Reid	Baird
Wilson	Schneberg	Seizinger
Hamby	Turner	Appel

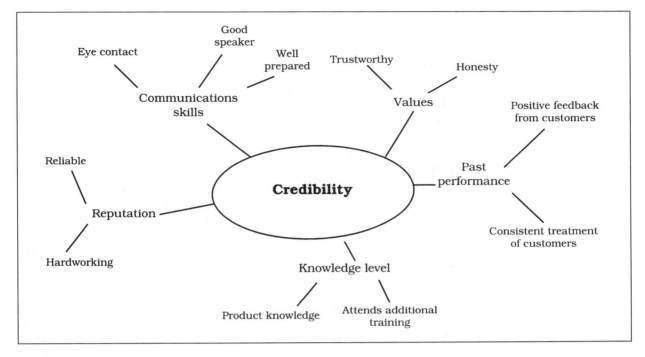

Figure 3.5
Mind Mapping

tant at this time in the mind-map. If visual images can illustrate ideas, it is appropriate to use them. Record as many ideas as possible. Review the ideas and make additions if any are suggested. Try putting aside your mind-map for an hour or even for a day and then review what you have written. Make any additions that you can. Then begin drawing conclusions from your "map." What possible solutions have been diagrammed that could possibly be implemented? Share your ideas with others and seek their feedback.

When mind mapping it is important to approach the exercise with an open mind and a willingness to think creatively. Mind mapping is not meant to be neat and orderly or even consistently realistic. It is meant to stimulate ideas and to help individuals consider what might be possible. Many people write speeches and plan meetings by creating mind-maps.

DEVELOPMENT OF NEGOTIATION SKILLS

When problems present themselves in a professional environment, often there are no easy solutions. Customer complaints, requests, or problems all must be resolved in an efficient manner. A constructive method of problem solving is to ask the customer what will resolve his or her situation. While this places responsibility on the customer, it also places a significant responsibility on the individual whose job it is to decide what an appropriate resolution would be. At this time the art of successful negotiation is necessary.

Negotiation is the evaluation of the possible solutions to a challenge and the selection of the solution that is mutually beneficial. Negotiation requires discussion between the two parties involved. It suggests that a resolution can be reached that everyone involved considers fair and reasonable. Negotiation must allow for give and take on both sides of an issue. To improve negotiation skills as a customer service provider, remember the following suggestions:

1. **Know your customer.** Anyone involved in solving a problem must know the parties involved. Past relationships can shed valuable light on how a customer may approach a current situation. New customers have unique qualities that we may have yet to discover. The more familiar we can become with our customers, the more likely that we will be able to recognize what their real problems or concerns are. Some customers may make outrageous requests initially, only to decrease their demands later. If this tendency has been determined previously, it is helpful to recall it as the negotiation process is beginning.

   Customers are unique individuals with their own sets of needs, motivations, and fears. The greater our awareness of these needs, motivations, and fears, the more effectively we can begin to solve their problems. Customers want to know that they are important to us and to our business. They also want to know that we remember them from one interaction to another. Any details that we can draw on about specific customers can help us to solve their problems appropriately.

2. **Ask questions and listen to the spoken and unspoken messages.** By asking questions of our customers and actively listening to their responses, we can develop an informed understanding of the situation at hand. The more information that can be collected, the more accurately we can help to solve the customers' problems. Customers are not always eager to share all the details of a situation. Effective questioning requires that the customer service provider continue to ask questions until he or she believes that all the pertinent information has been collected. Once questions have been answered, it is helpful for customer service providers to clarify their understanding by reviewing what they have interpreted from what the customer has shared.

   Customers may have unspoken messages that they are unwilling to share without some type of encouragement. Customers who are unable to pay their bills because of sudden changes in their lives may not feel comfortable sharing their problems with someone else. In this situation, the customer service provider must "listen" to what the customer is not saying. This can be done by listening to the hesitation that a customer may have in responding to a question, attempting to detect anxiety in the voice, or by asking nonthreatening questions that convey to the customer that meeting the current needs is of utmost importance. Although customers who are having cash flow problems may be reluctant to share the details of their situations, they will be pleased to learn about a company's special payment opportunities or other possible alternatives.

Sometimes asking a customer questions creates tension in a conversation. Customers may not want to share more information than they think is necessary. By asking well-presented questions, the customer service provider can create an environment in which the customer may be more willing to share the details that can lead to problem resolution. Questions must be asked with a tone of empathy. Customers need to know that they are important and that their best interest is the company's concern.

3. **Know the policies of your organization and in which areas flexibility is allowed.** When attempting to negotiate with customers, it is especially important to be very familiar with your company's policies. It is hard to coordinate a resolution to a situation if you are uninformed about what will be allowed. Not knowing company policies may make customer service providers appear unprepared or as though they have little or no authority. No customers want to hear that the reason that their requests cannot be granted is because it is against "company policy," but in many cases this is the only accurate response. Knowing what is not allowed is not enough. Customer service providers can go into a negotiation situation ready to negotiate if they also know what the policies allow. Unfortunately, all too often human beings focus on what cannot be done, rather than what can be done.

Most policies have been developed to establish a consistent method of responding to a common situation. In this respect, policies are a positive measure that prevent a company from being accused of showing favoritism among their customers. Customers may not always think of the existence of policies in this way. Customer service providers should know where and when flexibility is allowed with regard to policies. If customer service providers are trained and empowered, they will comprehend the amount of flexibility that they can exercise on behalf of their customers.

4. **Demonstrate the willingness to be flexible.** The ability to react to situations as they occur is important in demonstrating flexibility. It is not enough to want to give in to the customer's request; customer service providers must be able to convey that desire to their customers. By asking customers how they would suggest that a situation be resolved, an opening for their input has been suggested. If

their suggestions can be entirely or even partially implemented, the customers may feel that they have created a positive solution that the company was flexible enough to agree to. Flexibility can also be expressed through the words that are used in interacting with customers. Encouraging words that express appreciation for the customers' ideas are always a plus. Whenever possible, allow the customers to participate in the problem-solving and negotiation process. Their ideas may be inspired because of their involvement in the overall situation. Their approach to the problem resolution may be even more conservative than the one that the company might have offered.

5. **Learn to handle your anger and your customer's anger appropriately.** In a negotiation situation, anger is always a possibility. Something has taken the situation to the point of requiring negotiation. When anger is revealed, it is best to defuse it as subtly as possible. Anger may express frustration, anxiety, or unmet expectations. It may also be a result of a circumstance or circumstances totally outside the situation being discussed.

To diffuse a customer's anger, it is effective to anticipate the cause and to confront it carefully. The faster that anger is defused, the less likelihood that it will intensify. The customer service provider can acknowledge that a change in the situation could occur and then offer some type of compensation. A customer who is becoming angry because he or she has been waiting in line at a drive-up window at a fast food restaurant may angrily ask the manager what the holdup is. The manager may respond by saying that several employees called in sick and that they are understaffed. This response alone might make the customer even more angry, but when the manager offers free food or drinks to compensate for the customer's inconvenience, the anger may begin to diminish. By offering the apology and the free items the manager is acknowledging that his company is in error, but he is minimizing the effect of the error.

Whenever possible, shift responsibility for the customer's anger back to the customer. This must be done with care, but it can have positive results. A customer may phone his or her lawn care company, angry and ready to cancel the contract because of recurring weeds. When the company owner hears that the customer is concerned about the weed problem, he can immediately respond by saying that if the customer will call in the future, the company will provide an additional application at no cost. Although the owner does not say it, he is reminding the customer that it would be impossible for the lawn care company to re-check all customers' lawns to determine the effectiveness of each application. Encouraging the customer to share in the responsibility may defuse anger and allow the business relationship to continue. This approach could be effective if used occasionally, rather than frequently.

When customer service providers find that they are becoming angry, they should remember they are representatives of their company. Every individual must take responsibility for his or her own anger. A company's reputation will not be enhanced if employees allow their anger to be shown to customers. When you feel yourself becoming angry, move quickly to what can be done to resolve the challenging situation.

6. **Consider what the customer may lose in the negotiation process.** The nature of negotiation involves give and take. Customers may feel that they are doing all of the giving and that the company is doing all of the taking. Try to understand what the customer will see as a compromise. A customer who is delinquent in bill payment may be seeking to be relieved of some of the financial responsibility. Although this may be an unrealistic solution from the company's viewpoint, the customer may not see it that way. A modified payment schedule may be the solution to the situation, but the customer will still have to pay the bill. When negotiating with customers, stress that the goal is a positive resolution for all involved.

7. **Determine mutually beneficial solutions to challenging problems and situations.** When completing a negotiation with a customer, seek solutions that will benefit both the company and the customer. No one will gain if the customer leaves the interaction angry and vowing never to do business with the company again. Creating a win-win situation that both sides can live with makes potential future business relationships a possibility. Even if a company no longer wishes to do business with a customer, it must be remembered that possible business contacts with others who are acquainted with the difficult customer are probably desired.

Explain to the customer exactly how the agreed-upon solution will work. Seek feedback from the customer so that additional information can be provided, if necessary. Stress that the solution allowed both sides to compromise, but that the result will have a positive benefit for all.

PROFESSIONAL APPROACHES TO APOLOGIZING AND CONVEYING BAD NEWS As customer service providers attempt to assist their customers in problem solving, they may become aware of errors or oversights that were made by their own company, co-workers, or by themselves. Effective problem solving acknowledges the fact that the customers may have legitimate concerns and that the customer was treated inappropriately. If this is the case, the customer is due an apology. Apologies are not signs of weakness, but rather productive methods of continuing the opportunity to communicate.

Apologizing to customers is a reality of professional life. While customer service providers should not apologize without justification, they should be prepared to do so when appropriate.

When apologizing to customers, consider the following suggestions:

1. **Acknowledge the customer's feelings.** By indicating to the customer that we recognize their feelings and emotions, we send the message that we care.
2. **Express to the customer that you share the responsibility for the problem.** Even if you and your company were only loosely associated with the problem, you are a part of its diagnosis and resolution.
3. **Convey sincerity.** When apologizing to customers, it is important to convey care and concern. If we say that we regret that an error was made, the manner in which we say it should demonstrate our regret.
4. **Ask for the opportunity to correct the problem.** Just apologizing for a problem has little impact if we do not offer to correct the error or to make changes in the future. Saying to the customer, "May we correct the error for you?" expresses the desire to continue doing business with the customer.
5. **Request the opportunity to continue doing business in the future.** By asking the customer if we can still consider him or her our active customer, we suggest that we are willing to correct the error and would like to go forward in a positive business relationship. This request also gives the customer the opportunity to share other concerns which might keep him or her from doing business with us.

BARRIERS TO PROBLEM SOLVING AND DECISION MAKING

A number of barriers may exist that affect the actuality of problem solving and decision making. Frequently, decision makers are not aware that barriers are detracting from the decision-making process. Some of the most common barriers to problem solving and decision making are:

- **Resistance to change:** People are often reluctant to change from the time-honored way of doing things. Resistance to change can prevent people from taking chances and from considering new possibilities.
- **Habits:** Habits limit our vision of what can be accomplished, and sometimes stand in the way of solving problems. Habits may go undetected by an individual and may be a tremendous deterrent to correcting a problem. For example, a receptionist who is having difficulty completing his or her work may be unaware that the habit of taking personal calls is taking the bulk of work time.
- **Individual insecurity:** Individual insecurity may deter individuals from taking risks or from pursuing behavior that may require them to take a stand. Individual insecurity may come from past experiences or from an overall lack of self-confidence.

- **Past history:** Knowing what has happened before and what worked and did not work can inhibit an individual's desire to try new methods of problem solving or decision making. Past history is frequently an excuse for not making changes. The individual, who may not wish to approach a situation in a new way, may remind others that a similar idea failed in the past.
- **Fear of success or failure:** At some time, everyone experiences some type of fear. The fear of success or failure may be viewed as unreasonable, but it can greatly deter the confrontation of problems. The unknown can be a frightening thing. When a new way of doing something is attempted, it may work well or not at all. In either instance, changes may result. While some people thrive on recognition, others shy away from it. These fears may cause people to avoid the possibility of success or failure altogether.
- **Jumping to conclusions:** When problems must be solved and decisions made, it is easy to jump to conclusions. When someone jumps to conclusions, assumptions are made about what might or might not work or about the possible results; assumptions may frequently take on negative perspectives.
- **Perceptions:** As we have stated previously, perceptions are the ways that we see things based on our experiences. We may be unable to see something from another perspective because we are so blinded by our own perception.

By developing an awareness of some of the barriers to problem solving and decision making, customer service providers can attempt to overcome the barriers before they occur.

IMPORTANCE OF FOLLOW-UP IN PROBLEM SOLVING

Once a problem or problems have been solved or decisions have been made, it is vitally important to follow up. *Follow-up is checking back to determine whether or not a situation is operating according to the initial plan.* Effective follow-up requires that the original problem solver or decision maker check back with the customer to determine whether or not the original plan of action actually took place. The most effective approach to problem solving has little value if the solution was never fully implemented or if it has run into some type of difficulty. Customers remember the end of their interaction, not the beginning or the middle. A customer may have been treated in a friendly manner, had questions answered quickly, and been highly satisfied with a solution that was created to correct the problem; however, if for some reason the solution never took place, the customer will not remember the friendly treatment. The customer will remember that he or she still has a problem that needs to be resolved. Anytime a solution to a problem requires the involvement of someone other than the person making the commitment, follow-up should occur.

Keeping customers informed about the status of their order or problem even when there is no news to report can be an excellent public relations tool. A periodic call just to let the customer know that you have not forgotten them or their concern can be a refreshing change from the treatment that the customer may be accustomed to receiving. Their response may be, "I cannot believe that you called me back! Your company really does provide excellent customer service." Follow-up is a safeguard to ensure that customers continue to be satisfied with a company and the company's ability to meet the needs of its customers.

Through effective preparation, the reality of problem solving and decision making in customer service can become an active opportunity to convey to customers how valuable they are to the success of a business and that satisfying their needs is a part of the accomplishment of a company's goals.

SKILL BUILDING: PROBLEM SOLVING AND DECISION MAKING

Most customer service interactions require that problems be rectified and that decisions be made. Customer service providers have to equip themselves to be ready to analyze situations and to efficiently determine an appropriate solution.

Using the problem-solving strategies, determine your own solutions to the following "What would you do?" scenarios.

- The accounts receivable department that you manage has been having problems with customers not paying their bills on time. An additional problem is that numerous customers are sending the wrong portion of their bill with their payment. It has been suggested that the real problem is that the billing statement is in need of a new, more readable look.

  Applying one of the problem-solving strategies, determine the most appropriate solution to this problem.
- You have recently been feeling dissatisfied in your position as a reservation associate at a nationally recognized car rental company. There are opportunities for advancement at your current company, but you might like to look elsewhere for a new opportunity.

  Applying one or more of the problem-solving strategies, determine an appropriate direction to take.
- In your position as corporate trainer, you have noticed that many of your trainees/customers are not following through with the assignments that you give them and they frequently are not prepared for presentations when they are due.

  Consider the problem-solving strategies and use at least one to determine a solution to this situation.

OPPORTUNITIES FOR CRITICAL THINKING

1. Explain the problem-solving model and the seven steps to determining and implementing a solution.
2. How can brainstorming provide the opportunity for creative problem solving?
3. Why is it helpful for organizations to train their employees in possible approaches to problem solving?
4. How can the use of creativity in problem solving more effectively address unique situations?
5. A positive way to view problems is to think of them as opportunities. How can this approach reduce the temptation to respond defensively to a customer's problems or frustrations?
6. Discuss some guidelines to follow when encountering conflict.
7. Why is a simple approach to problem solving, like the use of pro/con sheets, frequently the most productive?
8. Select a problem or decision to be made and create a mind-map to explore possible solutions.
9. Why is an understanding of your company's policies important when negotiating a solution to a challenge?
10. How important is follow-up to the solution of a problem?

STRATEGY FOR FORMULATING A PLAN FOR SUCCESS

- **WHY A STRATEGY?**
- **PLANNING**
- **IMPORTANCE OF INFRASTRUCTURE**
- **CULTURE**
- **HIGH-TOUCH AND LOW-TOUCH CUSTOMERS**
- **SEGMENTATION OF YOUR MARKET**
- **DEVELOPMENT OF A STRATEGY**
- **SKILL BUILDING: TIME MANAGEMENT**
- **OPPORTUNITIES FOR CRITICAL THINKING**

REMEMBER THIS
*Quality is never an accident; it is always the result of
high intention, sincere effort, intelligent direction and skillful
execution; it represents the wise choice of many alternatives.*
WILLA A. FOSTER

WHY A STRATEGY? Excellent customer service is not an accident, but the result of a well-thought-out plan.

The most important step toward achieving excellent customer service is developing a strategy. *A strategy is a plan for positive action.* A plan is always necessary when attempting to accomplish goals.

A strategy can help a business to determine the proper level of customer service. If too much customer service is provided, it may create a financial problem. If too little customer service is provided, customers may take their business elsewhere.

Several variables must be considered when developing a customer service strategy: planning, infrastructure, culture, high-touch and low-touch customers, and market segmentation.

PLANNING When undertaking the challenge of developing a comprehensive customer service strategy, planning is the first step to take. To begin the planning process, customer service providers must establish goals to determine what they would like to accomplish in their customer service.

Planning is, in a broad sense, *finding a recognizable direction to focus on. More specifically, planning is the establishment of specific customer service goals.* These goals may vary from reducing customer complaints to answering customer calls in 20 seconds or less. Establishing customer service goals will help customer service providers to define what they would like to accomplish. It is not uncommon for additional goals or priorities to surface as the strategy is being developed.

IMPORTANCE OF INFRA-STRUCTURE Customer service is dependent on the existence of an appropriate infrastructure. *An infrastructure is made up of the networks of people, physical facilities, and information that support the production of customer service.* Frequently an organization will attempt to implement a customer service program without considering what the capabilities of its existing infrastructure are. For example, if a company adds a toll-free customer service hotline and does not increase the number of telephone lines into its business, it may do more damage than good to its customer service reputation. While adding the toll-free line was an excellent idea, the lack of extra lines may cause customers to become frustrated and hang up before their questions or concerns have been addressed.

One way of thinking of an infrastructure is that it is the "highway" that gets you where you need to go. Without a "highway," we don't always realize what is possible. Many cities find that if the city infrastructure (water, sewer, roads, electricity) does not keep up with population growth or population shifts, there are not adequate public services for the people. It is always interesting to see the new businesses that seem to pop up when a new road is built. In many cases the need for those businesses already existed, but because the infrastructure was lacking, they did not open.

Infrastructures require a lot of planning. If future needs are not anticipated, future costs may be greater. Very few infrastructure investments show a positive return in less than three to five years. The infrastructure should meet the needs of the customer. The largest cost of producing great service is creating the infrastructure to support it.

Infrastructure must be used to its fullest potential. If current technology is in place, but the employees have not been trained to use the technology, it is wasted. Unfortunately, this is apparent in all too many businesses. Numerous voice mail systems, computers, copiers, and fax machines are never used because the people to whom they were made available were never trained on them or never made the commitment to begin implementing their use. Today's customers use technology and they expect their customer service providers to use it.

As sales grow, the company's ability to serve its customers' needs should also.

CULTURE A customer service environment should have a customer service oriented culture. *Culture is composed of values, beliefs, and norms shared by a group of people.* Many people are not aware that every business has its own unique culture. All too often management preaches the importance of positive customer service, but then does not provide a work environment that allows that positive customer service to happen. If the "culture" does not encourage excellent customer service, excellent customer service will not exist.

EXAMPLES OF CULTURE IN SPECIFIC INDUSTRIES

1. Typical workday hours
2. Industry lingo
3. Peer accountability
4. Levels of certification
5. Extra company-sponsored activities

Southwest Airlines is recognized as a service provider with few customer complaints and consistent on-time performance. This is largely due to the customer service culture that they create for their employees. They encourage their employees to go above and beyond the call of duty. They allow their employees to dress comfortably yet professionally. Humor is an important part of the airline-customer relationship. Three ways that Southwest Airlines succeeds in creating a customer friendly culture are:

- **Practice the Golden Rule.** Do unto others as you would have them do unto you, both internally and externally.
- **View internal customers as number one.** Southwest believes that if you take care of the internal customers, they will automatically take care of the external customers.
- **Work hard, play hard.** Celebrate successes, offer incentives, and give people a reason to work hard.

**High-touch
and Low-Touch
Customers**

There are many different types of customers and customer services. Depending on several variables, customers will have different customer service expectations. One method of understanding customers is to classify them as high-touch or low-touch customers. *High-touch customers require a high level of customer interaction.* These customers come into their customer service experience expecting a high level of service. In most cases their perception is that the cost of providing the service is included in the price. If they do not experience a high level of interaction, they will probably be dissatisfied. The customer may not be capable of completing the interaction without assistance.

Examples of High Touch

1. Bank lobbies
2. Specialty stores
3. Hotel lobbies
4. Purchase of real estate
5. Lawyers and accountants
6. Prestige restaurants

When a choice is given, many customers choose a low-touch experience and may even resent being required to participate in a high-touch experience. *Low-touch customers expect a low level of customer interaction.* Low touch frequently exists because of technology. It tends to have high usage and low cost per use.

Examples of Low Touch

1. Pike passes (debit cards used on turnpikes)
2. Automatic teller machines
3. Express rental car checkout
4. Hotel bill viewing on television and express checkout
5. Pay-at-the-pump gasoline
6. Fast food drive-up windows
7. Do-it-yourself copy shops

If customers are satisfied with and even expect a low-touch experience, it is inappropriate to require them to participate in a high-touch experience. Customers have many reasons for taking advantage of low-touch customer services. A mother with small children may choose to go to the drive-up window at her bank because it is more convenient than unloading her children and going inside. If, upon arrival at the bank, she is told that her routine transaction must be completed inside, she may become discouraged and postpone completing it. If it happens often, she may change to a bank that will provide her with the convenience that she requires.

SEGMENTATION OF YOUR MARKET Understanding the similarities of your customers is important when developing a customer service strategy. *Market segmentation is dividing customers into groups with similar characteristics.*

Segmentation will help to divide customers into serviceable groups, making it easier to assess the appropriate services to provide. Segmentation can also identify unique customer groups with special needs such as health clubs with babysitting services or eye care clinics with available customer transportation.

Segmentation can also identify common customer service needs and less common needs. Segmentation is often difficult because of customer diversity, but it is an excellent starting point when developing a strategy.

SAMPLE CUSTOMER SERVICE SEGMENTS

1. Types of service needed or desired
2. Similarities among your current customers
3. Peak hours of your business and the specific customers doing business at those times
4. The amount of service desired
5. Creation of your own segments that are appropriate to your product or service

When the variables—planning, infrastructure, culture, high- and low-touch customers and market segmentation—have been evaluated, it is time to create a customer service strategy.

The following seven guidelines will provide a guide for creating the strategy.

DEVELOPMENT OF A STRATEGY

1. **Segment your customers.** Divide them into groups with similar characteristics.
2. **Identify the largest and most profitable customer groups.** It is better initially to serve the largest customer group, representing the majority of your business.
3. **Determine your customers' expectations.** Find out what your customers want from their experience with you.
4. **Develop a plan to achieve their expectations efficiently.** Create an innovative strategy that will allow you to serve your customers effectively.
5. **Implement the plan.** Put your new strategy into practice, implementing all aspects of the strategy at the same time.
6. **Set an evaluation timetable.** Before implementing your strategy, determine when an evaluation of its success will be conducted.
7. **Evaluate and continue to improve the strategy.** Evaluate the effectiveness of the new customer service strategy and make appropriate improvements. Keep making changes to keep the new strategy as current as possible.

SKILL BUILDING:
TIME MANAGEMENT

Time management is necessary for anyone who deals with customers. No one can improve your time management skills but you. If we have not done an effective job of managing our time, we will be more likely to become frustrated and to take our frustrations out on our customers. It is easy to let time slip away or to allow one customer to take the amount of time that would ordinarily be divided among several.

Time management must be ongoing and regularly practiced to make it a way of life. Ten tips for better time management are as follows:

1. Set goals and determine their priority.

2. Keep an updated calendar handy at all times.

3. Set tentative deadlines and reward yourself for meeting them.

4. Make a To Do list for the next day before you go to bed at night!

5. Take a break!

6. Focus on what must be accomplished.

7. Work SMART—not HARD.

8. Use the Swiss cheese method. (Break tasks into smaller pieces and work on them a little at a time.)

9. Evaluate. (Determine what is taking all of your time.)

10. Reward yourself for time well managed.

To evaluate your own time management complete the following exercise:

For three to five days, keep a log of how your time is spent. Record your activities, phone calls, breaks, etc. in accurate time intervals. Be honest about the time that you spend on all activities. Also, record whether the time was spent on a professional or personal activity. Analyze the amounts of time that you have spent on all of your different activities.

Divide the time spent into five categories: work-specific tasks, work-general tasks, personal-productive, personal-non-productive, and miscellaneous. Also include any comments that would clarify your activity or that you believe are pertinent.

SAMPLE TIME LOG

Start Time	Stop Time	Elapsed Time	Activity Code	Activity Description	Comments

Activity Codes

Work-Specific Tasks (WST)
Work-Generated Tasks (WGT)
Personal Productive (PP)
Personal Nonproductive (PNP)
Miscellaneous (MISC)

After tallying how your time was spent, attempt to draw conclusions about how you are spending your time. If more than 20 percent of your time at work is being spent on personal activities or 20 percent of your time at home is being spent on work activities, it may indicate that you are allowing each to spill over to the other.

Sometimes the conclusion that we are able to draw from keeping a time log is that unimportant activities are taking the majority of our time. Time management is an ongoing process. Try to use your time more appropriately; you may be surprised at the result.

If possible, share your time log with at least one other person. Ask those you share it with to suggest ways that you could better manage your time. Other people's ideas on how we can better manage our time can be helpful because we learn from their experiences.

OPPORTUNITIES FOR CRITICAL THINKING

1. Explain market segmentation.
2. Define culture and give two examples of culture in the workplace.
3. Explain the difference between high-touch and low-touch environments.
4. What variables should be considered when developing a customer service strategy?
5. Look for examples of infrastructure in your own organization.
6. Contrast the potential success of a strategy that is developed according to the guidelines for creating a strategy and one that is not.
7. Identify some customer service market segments that you are in.
8. Give examples of situations where high-touch and low-touch environments are appropriate.
9. What role do customers' expectations play in the establishment of customer service strategy?
10. Examine the culture of your own workplace.

EMPOWERMENT

REMEMBER THIS

Creative thinking may mean the realization that there's no particular virtue in doing things the way they have always been done.

ROGER VAN OECK

WHAT IS EMPOWERMENT?

As businesses continue to struggle to retain their current customers and to attract new ones, management is being required to look beyond traditional approaches. One new approach that has significant implications in the customer service industry is the idea of empowerment.

In customer service, *empowerment is to enable or permit customer service providers to make a range of decisions to assist their customers.* Customer service providers are continuously faced with customer situations that are unique to the customer and that are somewhere beyond the boundaries of the existing policies. Through empowerment, customer service providers are given the discretion to make decisions to further assist their customers.

Empowerment allows customer service providers to decide on their own whether or not customers' requests should be granted. Frequently, when customers have contacted a company with an inquiry, they have fully explained their situation to the person who is handling their call. If providers are truly empowered they can, within limits, decide how to resolve the situation. If the providers have to put the customers on hold or make them wait for an answer while the situation is explained to a supervisor, everyone loses. The customers have to wait and possibly retell their stories, the providers are taken away from their regular duties and feel like helpless middlemen, and the supervisor has to hear a hurried explanation of the situation. This scenario could be avoided through empowerment.

IMPORTANCE OF A MISSION AND PURPOSE STATEMENT

Empowerment is a philosophy that must be reflected in the culture of a business. The culture is composed of the values, beliefs, and norms shared by a group of people. In an "empowered culture," employees know the range of their power. They have been trained in the range of possible solutions to questions, and they know that their superiors are willing to live with their decisions.

All businesses that deal with customers should have an official *mission and purpose statement.* This statement expresses the *purpose (the reason for the organization's existence) and the mission (the means by which the organization will fulfill its purpose).*

EMPOWERMENT = OPPORTUNITY

Empowerment is a true opportunity. Customer service providers who deal with a large numbers of customers frequently know the solution to most common questions and problems. If they are given the power to deal directly with some of the more routine issues, more time is available to handle the more unusual situations and to be thorough with all of their customers. Empowerment also frees the time of supervisors who may be less productive because they continually have to deal with issues that could be handled more quickly by the customer service providers.

EXAMPLES OF EMPOWERMENT

At a local bank all bank tellers are given $100 each month to distribute among their customers. This money is used to compensate customers for being inconvenienced, for errors, or for having an especially long wait. The tellers can use this money as they deem appropriate. They can send the customers flowers, buy a steak dinner or tickets to a baseball game, or perform other goodwill gestures. The employees may not give any money or gifts to members of their families. They must document on an official form who the gifts were given to and why. The employees know that the bank customer may be contacted to confirm the donation.

Some utility companies are empowering their customer service providers by allowing them to hear a customer's situation and then grant them a special payment arrangement that will better meet the customer's current financial needs. The employees are also encouraged to send four cards to customers of their choice each day. These cards may recall something that the customer shared with the customer service provider, like the birth of a new baby or the purchase of a new home. The cards may also say "congratulations," "just a note," or "oops—we made a mistake." The intent is to create relationships with the customers, so that the customers feel that they have a real link with a person within the company.

Steps to Empowering Customer Service Providers

Empowerment does not just happen. It is the result of a company's focused efforts to establish guidelines, train employees, accept consequences, and celebrate positive results. When creating an empowerment program within your organization, consider the following recommendations:

1. **Paint a picture of what you hope to accomplish.** This "picture" can be an inspiring reminder of what your organization is trying to accomplish and how it can benefit each member of the organization.
2. **Allow workers to own their empowerment choices.** Give them responsibility that they can handle and give them feedback on their choices. Do not punish when mistakes occur, but instead retrain. Employees will avoid taking empowerment chances if they fear repercussions.
3. **Reward and recognize positive examples and results of empowerment.** You will show those in your organization that you are committed to the empowerment process.
4. **Commit for the long haul.** Positive results will not necessarily appear overnight, but they will be worth the wait!

Co-production of Customer Service

Another way of thinking of empowerment in customer service is to empower the customer. *Co-production is when customers participate in providing at least a part of their own service.* Customers are often willing and interested in participating in the customer service process.

EXAMPLES OF CO-PRODUCTION

1. Salad bars (make your own salad as you like it)
2. Free beverage refills that you get yourself
3. Self-service copy shops
4. Car washes valid for 7 days
5. College self-advisement (create your own schedule)
6. Completion of medical and insurance information while waiting for the doctor
7. Availability of your account number or medical chart number
8. Asking customers to complete deposit slips before going through the bank line and providing a place to do it
9. Telephone customer assistance lines
10. Payment at the pump for gasoline

A customer service system should be designed so that customers are allowed and encouraged to provide their own customer service. If everything else is equal, a system produces service more effectively when the customers participate as much as they can. (William H. Davidow and Bro Uttal, *Total Customer Service: The Ultimate Weapon* (1990). New York: Harper Collins.)

WHY CO-PRODUCTION WORKS

Co-production works because when customers participate in the process, they have some degree of ownership of the situation. In a manner of speaking, they have contributed to its success. Co-production also works because customers are not only contributing to the customer service experience, but also staying occupied instead of feeling like they are having to wait endlessly or are being imposed on. In addition, customer service providers have someone who is sharing the work and responsibility and they are therefore less stressed in successfully performing their jobs.

Co-production is not making the customer do all of the work. It is, instead, creating a partnership. Co-production is not abandoning your customers, being unwilling to assist, or letting the blind lead the blind. If a system is designed for co-production, but some element of the process is not in place, the system will fail. A business that requires the customer to fill out an order form in a store to complete a sale, but that does not have pencils or order forms available, will not succeed in empowering the customer. In this instance, co-production cannot succeed.

Co-production is not appropriate in every customer service situation or for every customer. In a prestige environment, it is inappropriate to expect that the customer will automatically want to participate in providing customer service. The customers may believe that they have paid (or are going to pay) someone else to do it.

The following are some techniques to help customers to become better co-producers:

- **Ask telephone callers to be prepared.** Have you ever wondered why you are placed on hold when calling in a mail order purchase and then a pleasant voice reminds you to have your catalog and credit card handy? The company is subtly reminding you to be a co-producer.
- **Repeat important information.** By asking customers to confirm their drive-up window order, mistakes can be corrected and customers can rethink their choices if they have a change to make.
- **Train customers to be co-producers.** Provide little things like simple instructions on a form to be completed, a prominently displayed sign indicating "express lanes" in discount stores, handing menus to customers waiting to be seated in restaurants, cart return areas in parking lots (along with a sign thanking customers for the cart return), and so on. When customers know what you expect of them, they can assist you more quickly and efficiently.
- **Tell customers why they should want to be co-producers.** If customers understand how everyone benefits from co-production, they are more likely to participate enthusiastically.

DESIGN OF SYSTEMS

Empowerment and co-production are two facets of customer service that do not happen automatically. They must be carefully included in a customer service system. *A customer service system is any set of procedures that contributes to the completion of customer service.* Not all customer service systems work efficiently and effectively. They must be designed to do so.

Unfortunately, many systems are in place because sometime in the past someone decided that a situation would be handled a certain way and no one has ever updated the procedure. Frequently, the person who has created a system is not the person who has to work with it. The best person in an organization to participate in creating a new system is the person who deals with it on an ongoing basis and who can see "the big picture."

If a question is repeatedly asked, or a process has more than a few steps, a system update may be needed.

GUIDELINES FOR SYSTEM DESIGN

The following six guidelines will help to create an effective customer service system.

1. **Identify** an area in need of a new procedure or a system update.
2. **List** the steps necessary to create or improve the system.
3. **Review** the mission and purpose statement to make sure that you stay on track with the company's goals.

4. **Seek to empower** those involved, both providers and customers. Eliminate unnecessary steps.
5. **Create a culture** that supports empowerment.
6. **Evaluate the system's effectiveness** after it has been in operation for a specified period of time.

<table>
<tr><td>

SKILL BUILDING:
CREATING CO-
PRODUCTION

</td><td>

Most organizations can meet a customer's basic needs. To be truly successful in the future, organizations must create an environment in which customer service is proactive and not mandatorily reactive. In a co-productive environment, customers are allowed and encouraged to participate in providing at least part of their own service.

Some of the requirements of co-production are:

- Co-production must create a partnership between the customer and the provider.
- Customers must have available the tools necessary to co-produce.
- Customers must know what their role in co-production is.

List some ways that you could create co-production in your own organization.

-
-
-
-
-

Share your new ideas for co-production with your co-workers or small group. Strive to sell others on the positive benefits of creating co-production!

</td></tr>
</table>

CHALLENGE 2

DESIGN OF A NEW SYSTEM

Customer service is more likely to occur when a well-designed customer service system is in place. Since many customer service systems are outdated or were created by individuals unfamiliar with the unique characteristics of a situation, a system update or review may be necessary. By learning how to create an effective customer service system, customer service providers are equipping themselves with the ability to initiate and request change.

CHALLENGE OBJECTIVES

1. To demonstrate an understanding of how systems can affect the success of a customer service program.
2. To implement the students' ideas in their own work environment (contingent on their supervisor's approval).
3. To successfully present to others the system developed.

ASSIGNMENT

Observe your work or personal environment. Attempt to identify an area of confusion or disorganization, or a system that in your opinion is just not working as well as it could be. Once you have identified this area, attempt to design an improved system to handle the challenge more effectively. Your system should include the steps necessary to better deal with the situation. Review the guidelines for creating an effective customer service system for additional guidance as you create your system. Also include a list of those who will be participating in the implementation of the new system.

PRESENTATION

Present your newly designed system in the form of a proposal. Include in your proposal:

1. A cover letter or memorandum introducing your proposal.
2. Explanation of the current system or lack of system.
3. Reasons why a system update is needed.
4. How the new system will improve efficiency.
5. How much you estimate it will cost to implement.
6. How you will train those affected by the new system to implement it.
7. An explanation of the system itself.
8. Any visual aids that further illustrate the system.
9. A summary paragraph that expresses the key aspects of the proposed system.

The success of your proposal will not depend on how intricate the system itself is, but instead on how well it is designed and how well you express your ideas on paper and communicate in written form.

Helpful hint: Take this opportunity to create a Microsoft PowerPoint presentation to share your proposal. If you have not previously worked with PowerPoint, ask a friend to help or just jump in. It is an easy-to-learn program and will greatly enhance your professionalism.

OPPORTUNITIES FOR CRITICAL THINKING

1. List three examples of co-production.
2. What are some guidelines for creating an effective customer service system?
3. How can a system update or the creation of a new system enhance the provision of excellent customer service?
4. What are some types of businesses that are most conducive to co-production?
5. Write a mission and purpose statement for your department or class.
6. Explain empowerment.
7. How can a lack of empowerment affect a customer service provider's ability to provide the service that customers expect?
8. Why are so many ineffective systems in place in organizations?
9. In your experience, are customers willing to provide a part of their own service? Why?
10. Why are individuals sometimes resistant to newly designed systems?

REMEMBER THIS

*Obstacles are those frightful things you see
when you take your eyes off your goals.*

UNKNOWN

WHAT IS COMMUNICATION? Customer service requires the ability to communicate effectively. *Communication is the process in which information, ideas, and understanding are shared among two or more people.* Frequently, individuals think that they are communicating, but the element of understanding may not be taking place. Customer service providers must develop their communication skills so that they are proficient in all methods of communication.

BUILDING CUSTOMER INTELLIGENCE The challenge of communicating effectively is made more difficult when providers do not have a good understanding of who their customers really are. One way to develop a more intimate understanding of customers is to build customer intelligence. *Customer intelligence is the process of gathering information, building a historical data base, and developing an understanding of current, potential, and lapsed customers.* Customer intelligence, or a customer IQ, allows organizations, specifically customer service providers, to better serve customer groups. It can help businesses to appropriately tailor services and service approaches to specific customers. Most business people today have recognized the importance of identifying why customers are more loyal to one organization than to others offering similar service or product opportunities.

Customer intelligence can enhance the possibility of improved relationship marketing. *Relationship marketing is cultivating a lasting mutually beneficial connection with customers.* Many businesses already have a considerable amount of information about customers at their disposal; they just have not recognized what can be interpreted from customer data. The methods by which customers chose to conduct business; the time of day they have questions; the depth of their expected interactions, purchasing patterns, expectations, and much more fall into the realm of customer intelligence. As with any personal or business relationship that we may have, the more we get to know and understand someone else, the better we can communicate with that person. The more positively and appropriately we approach our communication efforts with customers, the more likely that we will succeed in effectively serving them.

Customer intelligence takes market segmentation a step further. Remember, *market segmentation means dividing customers into groups with shared characteristics.* Customer intelligence examines not just today's customers but also lapsed customers. Finally, customer intelligence is continually being developed and being added to as new information or trends are discovered.

METHODS OF COMMUNICATION There are five main methods of communication used in effective customer service interaction.

1. **Listening:** The ability to hear and understand what the speaker is saying.
2. **Writing:** Communicating by using the written word so that others can understand the intended message.

3. **Talking:** Speaking, using words and terminology that others can comprehend.
4. **Reading:** The ability to read and comprehend the written word.
5. **Non-verbal expression:** Tone and inflection of voice, facial expressions, posture, and eye contact. Non-verbal communication can contradict the message conveyed through another method of communication.

All methods of communication are used in customer service. Customer service providers must continue to improve their communication skills. Different environments place emphasis on different methods of communication, but listening is thought by many to be the most important method of communication.

LISTENING To listen to your customers is to show them that you care about and respect their questions and concerns. It is not easy to be a good listener; it takes practice and dedication to improve your listening techniques. Listening is a skill that must continuously be developed.

Several barriers to good listening exist. Frequently a listener is distracted from what is being said, has a closed mind to the speaker and the message, won't stop talking, or is lazy and unwilling to make the commitment to be a good listener.

Many people believe that we have shorter attention spans because we have become so accustomed to commercial interruptions and to the pause button on our remote control—we find it difficult to pay attention to a speaker without allowing our minds to drift to other things. The best way to keep your mind focused on the speaker and to avoid becoming distracted is to pay attention. We can think about 10 times faster than we can speak, so frequently we have processed what speakers have said and are waiting for them to catch up with us. Focusing on the speakers and on what is being said makes us less likely to miss the messages being delivered.

We must also avoid becoming visually distracted. The clock on the wall, the cut on your finger, what is happening in the hallway, and your daily To Do List are all tempting diversions. Visual distractions may be very appealing because they require little effort to receive and may promote new ideas and thoughts, all of which take away from our ability to really hear what is being said.

The closed mind is a tremendous challenge to listening. No human being is without ideas, beliefs, and values. Those things that we think and believe may prevent us from really hearing what someone is saying. The temptation to jump to conclusions is usually present. A good listener must consider what is being said and avoid jumping to conclusions. When we open our minds to new ideas we have the opportunity to learn new things and to hear different perspectives.

Listening requires the listener to stop talking and hear what the speaker is saying. It is not uncommon for communication problems to arise when the speaker is trying to convey the situation, but the listener interrupts before the speaker is finished. It has been said that humans were given two ears and one mouth because we should listen twice as much as we speak. Putting that into practice is not as easy as it sounds. When listening to someone, allow the speaker to complete the thought before giving your response. Be an observer. Watch for pauses in the speaker's delivery that may indicate that the speaker is finished speaking. Also, wait until the speaker has stopped talking before you determine your response.

A good listener:

1. Conveys sincerity.
2. Doesn't interject his or her own thoughts.
3. Nods his or her head.
4. Doesn't finish the sentence for the speaker.
5. Paraphrases what was said.
6. Leans toward the speaker.
7. Shares positive comments.
8. Shows good eye contact.

To improve your listening skills try the following:

1. Focus on the speaker and what he or she is saying.
2. Look at the speaker and make eye contact when possible. If you are listening on the telephone, make notes as you listen.
3. Listen with an open mind.
4. Rephrase what was said to clarify that you understood the intended message.
5. Control your body language. Don't show impatience or disapproval.

A good listener knows the joy of sharing and communicating with others. Work to become the best listener you can be.

VOICE INFLECTION AS A CUSTOMER SERVICE TOOL Many communicators have a hard time conveying their spoken message to others. If others frequently ask you to repeat what you said, cut you off before you are finished speaking, or don't take you seriously, the problem may be the way you use your voice. *Voice inflection is variation in the pitch, timing, or loudness of the voice. Pitch is made up of the highs and lows of your voice.* A national study has shown that some of the most unpleasant voice characteristics of Americans are talking in a whining, complaining or nagging tone; using a high pitched, squeaky voice; using a loud, grating voice; mumbling; and fast-talking. Vocal problems are amplified by the telephone. Your voice and message reveal some very important characteristics about the person you are.

Some of the characteristics revealed are:

- Level of job satisfaction
- Attitude
- Gender
- Education
- Knowledge level
- Speed that you work and react
- Confidence
- The part of the country you are from
- Status
- Energy level
- Mood

Many people believe that our voices reflect our personalities. To illustrate the power of voice inflection, try the following exercise. Read the following sentence in your normal voice:

"John solved the software problem."

Repeat the sentence as a question, now as a secret, and now with surprise. The message conveyed using different voice inflection should have been different each time it was read. The voice inflection that we use can send different messages depending on where we place emphasis.

To improve your voice inflection try the following:

1. Tape yourself.
2. Ask friends for their honest assistance.
3. Make a conscious effort to improve.
4. Keep listening to yourself. It is easy to slip back into old habits. Excellent voice inflection takes practice!

TELEPHONES AND CUSTOMER SERVICE

Anytime you are on the telephone, you are selling yourself. A large percentage of customer service interaction takes place by phone. Due to this fact, customer service providers must have outstanding telephone skills. When communicating with customers by phone the advantages of face-to-face communication don't exist because there are no visual aids or body language. Instead, the communicator must depend on the listening skills, the ability to respond effectively to questions, and voice inflection.

The following are seven steps to answering a successful call

1. *Smile!* Your voice will sound friendlier if you have a smile on your face!
2. Answer the call with an *enthusiastic and professional greeting.* Your entire organization is depending on you to make a positive first impression.
   - Greet the caller.
   - Identify your organization or department.
   - Introduce yourself.
   - Offer your assistance.
3. *Ask questions* about anything that is not clear to you. If additional information is needed, ask for it and explain why it is needed.
4. *Give answers and assistance as quickly as possible.* If you can't solve the problem or answer the question, let the customer know what will happen next.
5. *Thank the caller.* Ask if you may be of further assistance.
6. *Conclude the call in a positive manner.* Think of every call as the beginning of a new relationship.
7. *Follow up the call* to make sure that the customer is pleased with the result and to make sure that everything you promised was delivered.

Organization is crucial when you interact with customers on the telephone. To become more organized, consider the following:

- Always have a notepad available. This is handy for making notes and jotting down the customer's name.
- Know the company's policies or have a reference close by.
- Tell the customer your name.
- Practice great listening skills.
- Check back with the customer to ensure that something was really completed.

WORDS TO USE/WORDS TO AVOID When dealing with customers some words are more positive and appropriate to use. Many of us use very negative and demeaning words when we speak with others. If we interact with customers we must rework our vocabulary so that we use words to create a positive environment.

Some customer service providers find it helpful to list Words to use/Words to avoid on a card so that it is available for easy reference.

POWER PHRASES By using power phrases we can send the message to our customers that they are very important and that we value their opinions. Here are 10 examples of power phrases.

1. Due to your specialized knowledge.
2. What a unique suggestion!

3. I'd like your considered opinion.
4. Please.
5. You are absolutely right!
6. If I could borrow just a moment of your time.
7. May I?
8. As you, of course, know.
9. I'd like your advice.
10. I would appreciate it if.

Using power phrases in our conversations with customers can express to them that their ideas are important. We also let them know that we recognize the value of their time and expertise.

POWER OF EYE CONTACT   Eye contact is always important when we are communicating with others. *Eye contact means allowing our eyes to make visual contact with someone else's.* Eye contact conveys sincerity and interest in our culture. If we avoid eye contact it may suggest a lack of concern or lack of honesty. Our eyes can also convey compassion and caring. Customers may perceive that a customer service provider is not interested in what they are saying if they do not periodically have eye contact with the customer.

Even when a customer service provider deals with customers by telephone, he or she must be concerned with eye contact because of interaction with internal customers.

WORDS TO USE	WORDS TO AVOID
• Please	• Can't
• Yes	• Never
• May I	• Don't
• Consider this	• You have to
• Do	• Don't tell me no
• Let's negotiate	• Won't
• Will	• Not our policy
• Thank you	• Not my job
• You	• Profanity
• Us	• Vulgarity
• Appreciate	• Problem
• Can	• Sorry
• Use their name	• Love slang (honey, etc.)
• Would you like	• We'll try
• Opportunity	• Haven't had time
• Challenge	• I don't know
• Regret	• Hang on for a second

When dealing with people from other cultures, customer service providers should be aware of cultural differences. In many other cultures eye avoidance is a sign of respect. Be sensitive to others but use eye contact whenever possible.

APPEAL TO THE SENSES IN COMMUNICATION

When attempting to communicate with customers, it is helpful to appeal to as many senses as possible. A waiter in a restaurant can create a dramatic picture of a food item if he describes it vividly for you and then shows it to you. He is appealing to your sense of sound, sight, and possibly smell. The combination creates more impact than appealing to just one of the senses. An example of this in customer service is when a customer has brought in a bill that he or she believes is incorrect; it would be helpful not only to show him or her the method of billing, but also to describe how it was determined. The more senses we appeal to the greater the possibility that customers will understand our message.

When customer service providers work exclusively on the telephone, they may appeal to additional senses by not only clearly explaining to the customer the answer to their concern, but also by providing written documentation of what was discussed. This documentation could be mailed as a follow-up to the phone conversation.

COMMUNICATION AND TECHNOLOGY

The customer service industry has been greatly impacted and enhanced by technological advances. Customer service providers must familiarize themselves with available technological opportunities. Three main areas of technology have emerged as being important to the customer service industry. Voice mail, fax machines, and electronic mail are actively in use on a day-to-day basis. Customer service providers must become proficient in using these technologies so that they can enhance their productivity and ability to serve customers efficiently.

VOICE MAIL

Most corporations have some type of voice messaging system in place. Customer service providers must be comfortable speaking with their customer's voice mail systems and must understand their own system.

Voice mail systems provide customers and customer service providers with wonderful opportunities for interaction. When customers are not immediately available, messages can be left to provide faster feedback. For customers, voice mail systems allow their calls to be answered faster; customers know that their calls will either be answered soon or that they can leave a recorded message detailing their situation.

When leaving a message on voice mail, use the following steps to increase customer responsiveness.

1. Speaking clearly and slowly, identify yourself, your company, the day and date, and the time.
2. State the reason for your call.

3. Suggest to the customer what the next step should be. Does he or she need to call you back or wait for more information?
4. Leave your name and the phone number where you can be reached. You have already given the customer your name, but in case he or she didn't write it down give it again with your phone number.
5. Close with a positive farewell.

Remember when leaving a recorded message that time may be short, so be as brief and to the point as possible.

Customers may become frustrated with having to talk to "a machine" when they have a question or problem. When answering complaints about voice mail, don't dismiss the complaint as being unimportant. Ask your customer questions so that you can find out what really went wrong. If the customer claims that the system is not working, call it yourself. The best way to find out how well something is working for your customer is to become the customer. If you find that something is malfunctioning in the system or that the system is awkward to work with, share the information with others who can make changes. Sometimes the problem is easily corrected. The music playing in the background may be too loud or may not be tuned in well; an out-of-date holiday greeting may be playing, or the voice on the recording may be irritating.

FAX MACHINES

Fax machines have become necessary fixtures in most offices, but surprisingly many people don't know the basic guidelines for using them. When using a fax machine, a fax cover sheet should always be used. A fax cover sheet should include several key pieces of information: your name, title, department, company, address, phone number, fax number, number of pages in your fax (including the cover sheet), and an introductory message. If the information you are faxing is of a confidential nature, it is appropriate to place a warning statement or disclaimer on the cover sheet also. The fax cover sheet is the first impression that the recipient has of your company. If your company does not have an official fax cover sheet, create one that includes all of the pertinent information and possibly your company logo. This does not take much effort, but the positive impression is long term.

When faxing information, strive for accuracy. Double check the number you are calling. A fax will not go through unless you reach another fax machine; it is unlikely that you would reach another machine if you dialed incorrectly, but it could happen. Make sure that the faxed information is readable. If the print is too small to read easily, enlarge it before faxing. If you have had difficulty in receiving responses after sending a fax, try using a broad tipped pen and writing ATTENTION or IMPORTANT across the cover sheet.

A faxed signature is in most cases considered as valid as a witnessed signature. This can really speed up the time it takes to do business, but it also places a considerable amount of responsibility on the parties involved.

Whenever possible, fax information after hours. Customers will be pleased because you won't be tying up their machine during peak usage; you will also save on long-distance costs. Finally, make sure that your fax machine is well-maintained and that it has an adequate paper supply. A difficult-to-read fax does not speak well of your company.

ELECTRONIC MAIL

Many businesses have incorporated electronic mail programs into their computer systems. Electronic mail, or e-mail, has in many cases eliminated the need for the paper memoranda that clutter employee's mailboxes, desks, and trashcans. It has also shortened the time spent on communication between people and departments. Electronic mail is probably most beneficial when we are interacting with our internal customers. A response that previously would have taken a few days to flow through the company mail system can now be delivered almost immediately. As with other communication technologies, electronic mail requires that the user understand how the system works.

When using electronic mail, users should become familiar with the usage policies of their organizations. There are several practices that are considered appropriate among all electronic mail users. The following are some of the most common:

- **Never type in upper case.** Using capital letters is considered poor etiquette and is harder to read.
- Remember to periodically **clean out your mailbox.** By cleaning out your mailbox you will be sure to discard old mail and will be reminded of what is current and pending.
- **Avoid sending personal messages over the system.** When you are communicating electronically you are usually using someone else's resource. You may also accidentally send your message to the wrong mailbox. Even a secured message can be broken into.
- Most E-mail can **ask for confirmation that the recipient has received the mail.** Use this feature whenever possible.

Electronic mail has added a new dimension to the challenges of communicating with both internal and external customers. Familiarize yourself with the system in your organization.

Developing excellent communication skills can give a customer service provider the best opportunity to communicate with customers in a manner that encourages understanding. The effective incorporation of the five methods of communication—listening, writing, talking, reading, and nonverbal expression—into our daily lives can provide us with the best means of communicating positively with our customers.

SKILL BUILDING: LISTENING

The need for outstanding listening skills is recognized by most customers and their service providers. One of the biggest obstacles to the development of effective listening skills is a poor self-awareness of our own listening abilities and habits.

Individually or in a group, have someone read the following story aloud. After it has been read, try to answer the accompanying listening comprehension questions from memory. Do not suggest that the listeners take notes, but they may if they initiate it. The reader should read at a normal pace.

Kendall needed to go to the store to pick up a few items for her dinner party. Before she left she decided to make a shopping list so that she would not forget anything. Unfortunately, she could not locate any paper so she wrote her list on a sack from the 5 & 10 Drug Store. The first item she listed was lettuce, but two heads or one? One would be sufficient. She also needed steaks. Of the eleven people she had invited, only eight had responded to the invitation. Kendall's friends Jacob and Andrew did have a reputation for just showing up so she determined that she should buy food for two extras.

This meant that she should buy ten steaks. She also needed potatoes, carrots, bread, milk, sour cream, green beans, and two dozen eggs. Kendall considered garnishing her salad with tomatos, but decided against it. She thought that her list was complete, but looked in her refrigerator to be sure. One final item that she needed was strawberries for the dessert. Off to the store she went.

Try to answer the following listening comprehension questions, recalling the story that was just read.

1. Who was having the dinner party?

2. How many had confirmed that they were coming to the party?

3. What was on the shopping list?

4. What was the list written on?

5. What type of meat was being served?

Check your answers with the story. If you answered correctly, you are probably a good listener. If you were unable to respond accurately to the questions you may need to begin to work on improving your listening skills.

Complete the following listening self-assessment to evaluate yourself as a listener.

1. List four of your best qualities as a listener.

2. List four of your most common listening weaknesses (mind wanders, etc.). Rank them from worst to best.

3. How long is your average attention span?

4. List four qualities of outstanding listeners.

5. List any outside distractions that interfere with your ability to be an effective listener.

Examine the answers that you gave to the listening self-assessment questions. Now that you have identified your listening strengths and weaknesses you can begin to establish an action plan to become a better listener. Write three specific goals that you can work toward to improve your listening and a timetable for the accomplishment of your goals. Outstanding listening skills can be the determining factor between an average customer service provider and an outstanding one. Happy listening!

OPPORTUNITIES FOR CRITICAL THINKING

1. List four words to use and four words to avoid.
2. List and define the five methods of communication.
3. What factors can cause people to have poor listening skills?
4. What characteristics can an individual's voice reveal?
5. Explore some tactics for recording information received by telephone. What procedures does your company use?
6. How can the development of customer intelligence enhance relationship marketing with specific clients?
7. How should you respond if a face-to-face customer refuses to maintain eye contact?
8. How do you view voice mail systems as a customer? As a customer service provider?
9. What information should be included on a fax cover sheet?
10. Investigate the privacy issues related to electronic mail.

COPING WITH CHALLENGING CUSTOMERS

- WHO ARE CHALLENGING CUSTOMERS?
- WHY ARE CUSTOMERS CHALLENGING?
- ARE YOU CREATING CHALLENGING CUSTOMERS?
- CHARACTERISTICS OF CHALLENGING CUSTOMERS
- RESPECT: A CLASSIC IDEA THAT STILL WORKS!
- UNDERSTANDING THE POSITIVE POWER OF EMPATHY
- RESPONSIBILITY CHECK
- WHAT TO DO WHEN YOU ARE WRONG
- SIX SUPER WAYS TO COPE WITH CHALLENGING CUSTOMERS
- THE PAYOFFS OF COPING WITH CHALLENGING CUSTOMERS
- SKILL BUILDING: COPING WITH CHALLENGING CUSTOMERS
- OPPORTUNITIES FOR CRITICAL THINKING

REMEMBER THIS

*Nothing gives one person so much advantage as to
remain cool and unruffled under all circumstances.*

THOMAS JEFFERSON

WHO ARE CHALLENGING CUSTOMERS?

As we interact with others in our daily lives, we become painfully aware of the fact that some individuals are easier and more enjoyable to be around and to spend time with than others. Those individuals who, for one reason or another, "bother" us are the people that we probably attempt to avoid. Unfortunately, in business, we cannot avoid our customers. In fact we are frequently required to spend the most time with those customers that we find the most challenging.

Who are challenging customers? *Challenging customers are those customers with problems, questions, fears, and personalities that require us to work to achieve true communication.* Because all individuals have their own unique personalities and sets of past experiences, all individuals will not find the same customers challenging. In spite of the fact that challenging customers may be difficult to interact with, the reality is that they are still our customers and our overall goal is to provide them with excellent customer service and a feeling of satisfaction with their experience.

WHY ARE CUSTOMERS CHALLENGING?

Customers may be seen as challenging for a wide variety of reasons. They may have personalities or communication styles that we personally find difficult to interact with. Thus customers may be seen as challenging without having done anything specific to us. Customers may be perceived as challenging for any or all of the following reasons:

- They do not speak your language.
- They do not have expertise or an understanding of the specific product or situation.
- They may be openly hostile.
- They are visibly upset about something (and it may not have anything to do with you or your company).
- They are very quiet and non-communicative.
- They show an attitude of superiority.
- They are impatient.
- They imply that they are doing you and your company a big favor by doing business with you.
- They appear to embody the type of person that you have a personal bias against.
- They are so nice that you hate to have to give them bad news.
- They are extremely angry.
- They have difficulty in making decisions.

Everyone is someone's challenging customer. Customers want to believe that they are the most important persons in our lives at this moment. As we strive to provide excellent customer service, every customer should be the most important person at the moment. Challenging customers are never challenging by accident. They come into our interactions with past experiences, perceptions, expectations, frustrations, the stresses of daily life, and the desire that we show that we value them as our customers. Customer service providers also bring their own unique sets of ideas to an interaction. The difference between the two is that the customer service provider has the responsibility of building the bridge of communication.

ARE YOU CREATING CHALLENGING CUSTOMERS? Some customers are just challenging, no matter what we do or do not do for them. Most individuals who work with the public believe that they do a good job of interacting with their customers, but in reality we may create many of the customer problems that we experience. While we should be thankful for the customers who are for the most part happy and cooperative, our mannerisms or comments may "rub them the wrong way" or really offend them and cause them to become irritable or uncooperative.

Five tips to avoid creating challenging customers are as follows:

1. **Respect the customer's time.** Always work at peak efficiency. It is easy to fall into a laid-back manner of dealing with people we feel comfortable with. Stay focused on the customer.

2. **Do not impose your bad or negative mood on anyone else.** Everyone has a bad day once in a while but customers should never be able to tell that you are having a rough day. Both customers and customer service providers have problems, but customers do not enter into the customer experience to hear what is going on in your life. People will avoid dealing with you if you earn the reputation of being moody or having up and down days. Do not neglect your interactions with your internal customers. It is not enough to be nice to your external customers and then to treat your co-workers in negative ways. Frequently if you immerse yourself in doing your job and being positive, you will forget what was bothering you and will have a better day than you expected.

3. **Recognize regular customers with a smile and try to learn their names.** Customers must value the experience they have by doing business with your organization. It is not too much to expect you to remember them from one interaction to another. Giving someone a look of recognition is a great place to start. Recognizing customers starts with deciding that you are going to make the effort to do it. Everyone feels more welcome and a part of things if they think that someone else recognizes them. Try for one week to call everyone possible by name, including your internal customers, and you will see positive results. You may increase the morale in your work area and you will end your workday feeling like you have a lot of new friends. People usually choose to do business with people that they like!

4. **Avoid destructive remarks.** Insults, little "zingers," that may give you the satisfaction of having the last word, make you feel like the

winner now. In the long run they will make you the big loser. Some customers may seek ways to get back at you and others may avoid you and your company because they were hurt or assume that the entire organization is as rude as you were. The Golden Rule is a good one to follow in this situation. If you would not want someone to say it to you, do not say it to them. In the long run, destructive remarks are just that, destructive.

5. **Show initiative.** Show the customer that you are willing to complete a task or go the extra mile. Laziness abounds in our society today. What a refreshing change to do business with someone who offers to do a little something extra or to carry through a project to the end. Most customers do not expect to work with someone with initiative, so you will be a hero in their eyes.

Challenging customers can be categorized in many different ways. The following are 10 characteristics of challenging customers. Remember, challenging customers are frequently challenging because of who we are, not who they are.

CHARACTER-ISTICS OF CHALLENGING CUSTOMERS

1. **Language and/or cultural barriers:** As our society continues to include people from other cultures, we will increasingly come into contact with individuals who speak English as a second language or who barely speak English at all. Communication can be challenging, even when we speak the same language. When attempting to communicate with others who have difficulty with English, speak slowly and clearly. Always avoid using slang terms that are hard to translate. If words are not conveying the intended message, try illustrating with hand motions. Don't pretend that you understood what the customer said if you didn't. Ask questions and repeat what you understood. Try not to become frustrated. Even customers who have a hard time understanding our spoken message deserve patience. They are still our customers. Sometimes writing out the message makes it easier for a non-English speaking person to understand, because they can refer to their dictionaries. Keep an appropriate language dictionary handy so that you can clarify what they are saying.

   If all else fails, suggest that the customer call back or come back with an English-speaking friend who can help resolve his or her situation. Identify the most common languages that are dealt with in your business in your part of the country. The languages that these customers speak might be appropriate languages for you to begin to learn. Many customer service oriented companies require fluency in specific languages as a condition for employment.

Some individuals offend others from other cultures out of ignorance. Learn about the cultures of your customers. Information is readily available and all will benefit from the insights into customer's native traditions, ways of doing business, concerns, and beliefs. America is a melting pot of unique individuals with something to offer and with dollars to spend—either with our organization or someone else's.

2. **Older customers:** American society is getting older. As this fact becomes more and more apparent, it becomes important to recognize the reality of older customers. First of all, what does it mean to be older? Different people will give different responses. For our purposes, older customers will be defined as those customers who are 65 years of age and older. This is a significant percentage of the American population. The stereotype of an older person as one who is incapable of making decisions and having little discretionary income are ideas of the past. Today's 65+ customer is independent, active, self-sufficient, and living life to the fullest.

When dealing with older customers, customer service providers must remember to treat them with respect and attention. Their purchasing power is extremely significant. Older customers may require some special attention. They may have some trouble reading fine print, may have a slightly slower response time, or may be slightly hard of hearing. When interacting with an older person, always show a high level of respect. Recognize the individual's need for self-respect. While many older customers are pleased to find that they are eligible for senior citizen discounts, some may not appreciate being informed that they qualify. Never talk down to an older person by referring to them as "little lady" or "young man." Although you may be trying to warm up to them, such expressions just call more attention to them.

If you notice that a customer is having difficulty in reading, suggest that they move to a better-lit area; if they are still having difficulty, offer to read the information to them. Many older people have trouble hearing. A simple approach for helping them to understand what you are saying is to look at them while you are talking so that they can see your lips moving. Don't shout, as this draws undue attention. Do speak clearly, at a moderate pace, and do not mumble.

Older customers may be unfamiliar with some current technology. This is certainly not necessarily the case, but it may be. If a customer is not currently in the workforce and does not work with items such as computers, fax machines, and cash registers, they may find them overwhelming. On the other hand, some older customers may be much more proficient than we are because they have invested time in learning new technologies. If a customer seems to be unsure of how to use equipment, ask if you may be of assistance. If they accept your offer, assist them in a positive manner. If they refuse your offer, allow them to figure it out for themselves.

3. **Impatient customers:** People today operate at a fast pace. As we go about our daily personal and business lives, we are often attempting to accomplish many tasks within a short amount of time. Often the challenge is not attainable. Our customers are attempting to do the same thing. The rush to fit everything in can cause customers to become impatient. When customers are impatient or irritable, it is important to remember that they may be bothered by something beyond our control—a traffic snarl, a headache, or a dread of completing the task at hand. There are times when their impatience is because of something we have done or because of an antiquated system of doing business.

When calling customers on the telephone, always ask if you are calling at an appropriate time. A customer who is in the middle of doing something important is likely to express his or her impatience and may be distracted as we talk. Stress to your customers that your goal is to work with them as efficiently as possible. Tell them that you have their interests in mind. Stay on the task at hand and complete their business quickly and accurately. Impatient customers may complain that you are disrupting their work or are a bother to them. Strive to show the impatient customers, through your actions, that your company is worth the investment of their time.

4. **Angry customers:** Unfortunately, anger is a common emotion in customer service. Both internal and external customers experience anger from time to time. Anger among internal customers, if improperly managed, can create an all-out war between departments—a situation that does not promote easy internal customer service in the future.

The only time that many external customers call with customer service challenges is when they are angry. Anger can be like dynamite waiting to explode. If not properly defused, it can cause quite a commotion.

To respond to a customer's anger, try to calm the customer. It is important for the customer service provider to stay calm. Angry customers have the ability to bring out anger in everyone with whom they come into contact. Ask the customer to explain his or her situation. Allow customers to vent their situations and feelings. They will feel better when they get it all out. Do not interrupt them; let them finish, and then respond. Acknowledge the customer's emotions, but find out the facts. As the customer is explaining, he may be losing some of his original fury. He or she has found someone who is willing to listen. Attempt to find effective solutions to the situation.

Angry people can become abusive or may resort to the use of profanity. This puts the customer service provider in a difficult situation. Should he or she take the abuse or stop it and risk making the customer even angrier? One response to a customer's use of vulgar language is to say, "I realize that you are upset, but I am not used to being spoken to in this way, please limit your explanation to the facts." Always approach customers with respect, even when they are behaving in an unprofessional manner. Acknowledge their emotions, but as quickly as possible, look for an opening to gain control of the conversation. Phrases like: "I recognize your frustration . . . " or "let's find a positive conclusion to this situation" are lead-in sentences that may allow the customer service provider to take charge. Customer anger provides the opportunity for a new relationship to begin and can have a positive result.

5. **Analytical customers:** Customers who are analytical tend to have a need for facts and like to know that they are speaking with someone who is knowledgeable about his or her product or company. They frequently take an objective approach to decision making and to problem solving. Analytical people rarely show their emotions and are not concerned about your emotions. They are not concerned with whether or not you like them.

   Analytical customers like consistency and proof. When dealing with customers who want facts and definite answers, treat them with respect and give them what they want. Tell them how a bill was figured, what the billing dates are, when the interest rate is going up, and anything else that they ask that you can give a factual response to. Ask them if they have additional questions and answer them efficiently.

6. **Noncommittal customers:** Some customers have difficulty in making decisions. They may be unwilling to commit because they are seeking information from several sources, or they may be hesitant in making a decision. Individuals seem noncommittal for a variety of reasons. They may have been too quick to commit to one option in the past and then have regretted their choice. They may have financial constraints that require them to carefully survey all options and determine the short-term and long-term feasibility of a decision. Other customers may have to consider the expectations of their superiors or co-workers who are not present but who will also benefit from the decision.

   When interacting with noncommittal customers, keep in mind that customers are not slow to decide because they want to frustrate you. They have their own reasons why they are hesitant to commit. To help them to a speedier decision, detail the possible options. Ask if there is anything that you have not explained. Suggest that they make a decision today. If they are not ready to do this, suggest a timetable that would allow a moderate amount of time for their consideration of a decision. The timetable will give them a deadline to work toward and will diminish the possibility that the information you have shared with them will become out of date.

7. **Superior customers:** Some customers may present to the customer service provider the impression that they are in some way superior. It is important not to take this type of attitude seriously. Customers who show an attitude of superiority can be frustrating to interact with. They may be rude or make condescending remarks. In reality, customers who present themselves in this manner are frequently insecure and feel as though they can somehow seem better if they put someone else down. They want you to know how important they consider themselves.

   When dealing with this type of customer, the customer service provider must recognize his or her own self-worth. The temptation is strong to enter into a competition with the customer to see who really is better, but this only proves to be an unproductive waste of time, and no one really wins in the end. When possible, use the customer's attitude of superiority to your advantage. Praise his or her accomplishments and importance. Suggest that your resolution of the situation will enhance his or her position. By helping the customer to see that he or she will be the winner in the end, the competition can be reduced.

8. **Immature customers:** Most customer service providers have the opportunity to interact with many immature customers. A great deal of customer service centers around problem solving, and immature customers are likely to have some problems. Late or unpaid bills, excuses, and blaming others for their problems are common occurrences for immature customers. When interacting with immature customers, listen to their explanation of the situation before responding. Allow them to fully describe their problem or question. When responding, be frank about the consequences that may result from not paying bills and other similar dilemmas. If they have questions, answer them fully. Your perception may be that they are asking something that "everyone knows," but they apparently don't if they are asking. Immature customers need to know that their actions affect others. Stress the importance of your company policies and the need to treat all customers fairly and consistently.

   Immature customers may really not know any better than to act and react in the manner that they are sharing with you. Customers who complain about having to pay a large utility bill on time and say that if they pay it, they will not have any money left to go out to eat probably need a "reality check." Be firm with them. They may not appreciate your enforcing your company's policies now, but they will learn from the experience.

9. **Talkative customers:** Talkative customers can be exciting to be around. They may be outgoing and may have interesting stories to tell. They are often good storytellers and may secretly enjoy hearing themselves talk. In spite of the fact that we may sometimes enjoy being around talkative people, we must still conduct business efficiently. Some talkative customers are difficult to be around.

   When communicating with talkative customers, approach them in a positive and open manner. Allow them to share their questions or concerns. Help them to stay on the subject by asking specific questions that further explain the situation. Express your interest in rectifying their circumstances. Show appreciation for their knowledge and abilities. Operate at a fast pace, use humor to keep the discussion focused, and ask them if they have further questions. Conclude by expressing appreciation for their patience and understanding. It is sometimes difficult to end conversations with talkative customers; try a phrase that suggests that they are on a time schedule. "I don't want to take any more of your limited time" may be an effective closing.

10. **Customers with special needs:** Customer service providers may have some customers who require additional assistance because of a special need. Special needs customers include all customers who require our productive cooperation. It is difficult to truly define who a special needs customer may be since many individuals who are viewed by society as having special needs do not perceive themselves in this way.

    The American Association of Retired Persons (AARP) offers some suggestions for communicating with someone with a disability.

    If a person . . .

    . . . Is visually impaired. Never pet or play with a guide dog; you will distract the animal from its job.

    . . . Has a speech impediment. Be patient, listen attentively, and resist the temptation to finish his or her sentences.

    . . . Is in a wheelchair. Sit down, if possible, so you can chat eye to eye. Do not touch the wheelchair (or similarly, someone's crutches or cane), because it is considered within the boundaries of an individual's personal space.

    . . . Has a hearing loss. Always speak directly to the person, not to her interpreter or assistant if one is present. If you raise your voice, it becomes distorted and even more difficult to understand. Just speak clearly and slowly, facing the person. People who are deaf depend a lot on facial expressions and gestures for communication cues. Additionally, you should never assume that someone needs or wants help—but do not be afraid to inquire politely. For example: "I hope I do not offend you, but may I be of assistance?"

As always, customers with special needs should be treated with respect. Strive to understand their questions and concerns, and attempt to provide appropriate solutions.

RESPECT: A CLASSIC IDEA THAT STILL WORKS!

As our society becomes more focused on the unique differences among individuals of different ages it is easy to fall into the "generation gap syndrome." This is the idea that individuals who grew up at different times and shared different life-shaping experiences cannot ever really communicate. This could not be a more incorrect notion! People of all ages can communicate and coexist peacefully, but the necessary ingredient is respect. *Respect is to give someone recognition or special regard.*

To respect and to show respect for someone else does not minimize our own self-worth. Instead it allows the opportunity for us to learn from someone else and to grow in ways that we would not if we only interacted with those just like us. The need to show respect is not limited to those in a different age group, but should be shown to all others. By using courtesy titles like "Sir," "Ma'am," "Mr.," and Mrs.," we show professionalism and demonstrate the regard we have for the other individual as our customer. If a customer does not desire to be addressed this formally we should follow through with their wishes. Never show condescension. Talking down to customers, even *very* young ones, only makes them feel uncomfortable and may make them angry. There is also the implication that customers are unable to understand the information that we are sharing with them. Finally, show respect for the knowledge that the customer has. Customers today are better informed and more sophisticated than they ever have been in history. Age, sex, race, education, etc. have no real bearing on what a customer may have an in-depth knowledge of. If we allow ourselves to recognize the knowledge of our customers, we will benefit and end up learning from them.

UNDERSTANDING THE POSITIVE POWER OF EMPATHY

Empathy is the ability to understand what someone is experiencing and to take action to assist in resolving the situation. Empathy is productive. When we show someone empathy, we do not express our sorrow over their situation. Instead we listen to their explanation of the situation and say, "What can we do to help you?" The main focus of empathy is problem solving.

If a customer calls to say that he or she is late paying a bill because there was a death in the immediate family, he or she has obviously suffered an emotional experience. By showing empathy, we convey that we are sorry to hear of the loss and would like to minimize stress if we can. Perhaps we can arrange an extended due date for the billing, or arrange for special financing. In either case the customer service provider is helping the customer to resolve his or her problems rather than dwelling on them.

RESPONSIBILITY CHECK Businesses walk a fine line with regard to customer service. In most cases, a business has what the customer wants and needs, but a business must be managed with profitability in mind. Sometimes a customer will make an unjustified request for service. This request may put the customer service provider and the business in an awkward position. Should the customer service provider provide the service and risk profitability or refuse to provide the service and risk losing a customer?

One method for dealing with this type of situation is to perform a responsibility check. *A responsibility check is assessing a situation and determining who should have responsibility and who really does have the responsibility.* Sometimes a customer is unhappy with us for not doing something that was really his or her responsibility. To provide excellent customer service, the customer must be permitted to participate in the process and not just benefit from it. Accountabilities must be created and enforced.

An example is a situation in which a responsibility check is appropriate between a student and a professor. In an educational setting the students are the customers and the professor is the customer service provider. The overall goal is to provide the student with the opportunity for learning with the positive outcome of a good grade. The professor needs to keep his or her students satisfied so that they will continue to enroll in classes, but at the same time he or she must strive to maintain the integrity of the course and institution for all students. If a student/customer who has not attended class and who is not succeeding approaches his or her professor and suggests that since the student is the customer the student should receive a good grade for the class, the professor must perform a responsibility check. Whose responsibility is it to enable the student to earn a good grade? It is a joint responsibility of the professor and student. The professor must provide pertinent information, be available to answer questions, and test fairly. The student must attend class, read the textbook, and study. The student was not living up to his or her responsibility. If the student is not making the necessary contribution, it would detract from the integrity of the course if the professor gave the grade that the student wanted. When providing customer service, all customers must be considered, not just a few.

The goal in performing a responsibility check is to clarify what went wrong in a situation and to shift the responsibility to the responsible party. The shifting of responsibility can be enhanced by co-production of customer service. The responsibility check is a positive approach to creating the opportunity for excellent customer service by requiring all who are involved to participate in the process and to take responsibility. Responsibility checks must be handled tactfully, but they can create opportunities for better customer service to all customers.

WHAT TO DO WHEN YOU ARE WRONG As a customer service provider interacts with his or her customers, the possibility exists that he or she will not treat all customers as well as they should be treated. Customer service providers are only human and may be tempted to take out their frustrations on their customers or they may make mistakes. When you believe that you have treated a customer inappropriately, try the following:

- **Review the situation.** Examine your behavior and the words that have been spoken. Try to look at the situation from the customer's point of view.
- **Observe the customer's reaction.** Is the customer visibly upset? Does the customer seem surprised or hurt by your actions?
- **Admit the mistake.** Whether or not it was an error in your information or judgment, it is always best to acknowledge that you are aware of it.
- **Apologize for your actions or error.** Express to the customer that you regret the problem, but do not make excuses.
- **Find a solution and implement it.** The most effective way to undo the improper treatment of a customer is to create an effective solution and to put it into effect as quickly as possible.

SIX SUPER WAYS TO COPE WITH CHALLENGING CUSTOMERS

1. **Listen.** Allow customers to express their concerns or to share their side of the story.
2. **Ask questions.** Seek clarification of the problem. Determine the variables involved.
3. **Show empathy.** Attempt to understand what the customer is experiencing and take action to assist in resolving the situation.
4. **Solve the problem.** Determine the most appropriate solution to the situation. Use creativity and follow company policies as you seek to create a positive outcome for both the customer and your organization.
5. **Follow-up.** Restate what has been decided and how the situation is being resolved. Ask the customer if he or she has any more questions.
6. **End on a positive note.** Thank customers for their understanding. Bid them farewell in an enthusiastic manner so that they remember the professional manner in which you resolved their problem. Customers are more likely to remember the end of an interaction than the beginning.

THE PAYOFFS OF COPING WITH CHALLENGING CUSTOMERS

Customer service providers must think of their customers as long-term assets! Keeping in mind that it is much easier to retain an established customer than it is to recruit new customers, the customer service provider should be extremely motivated to resolve challenging customers' problems. Customers should be made to feel better at the end of an interaction than they felt at the beginning. It is easy to take care of customers when things are going well; it is when things become challenging that difficulties may arise.

We learn to deal with conflict by confronting it. When we require ourselves to develop skills or to learn new information, we are creating an environment where we can become better at managing conflict. Challenging people are a reality of customer service! Knowing how to handle them appropriately can reduce both our customer's stress and our own. By learning to cope with challenging customers, we become more valuable assets to our company and the job that we were hired to perform.

Skill Building: *Coping with Challenging Customers*

Customers may be challenging for a variety of reasons. In some instances, the customer is doing nothing to challenge us other than just being themselves. Challenging customers are a reality of professional life, especially in the customer service industry.

One of the best methods of becoming more comfortable with challenging customers is to practice. Resolve the following "What would you do?" scenarios.

- In your job as a receptionist in the international affairs department you have the opportunity to interact with numerous people each week. Even though you consider yourself to be a good communicator you sometimes feel frustrated as you attempt to communicate with some of your non-English-speaking customers. What can you do to improve your skills in communicating with these challenging customers?

- You work in the order confirmation department of a large catalog company. Part of your job responsibility is to call suppliers to confirm the ship dates for ordered goods. You spend your entire day on the telephone and for the most part enjoy your job. Your only real frustration is when you call a few of your customers and they react impatiently and rush to get off of the phone. What can you do to improve your skills in communicating with impatient customers?

- In your position of residential services coordinator at a major telephone company you encounter customer problems and concerns daily. While most customers state their situation and are open to your information and knowledge, you do have one type of customer that you find to be challenging. Today, you had a call from a customer who was angry about receiving a cancellation notice from your company due to non-payment on the account. As you discuss the situation, the customer tells you that they think that it is unfair to expect a payment every month and that your rates are too high. They go on to tell you that if they paid their bills in full and on time they would not have any money left over to eat out. You recognize that this customer lacks maturity; how do you respond appropriately to this customer and others like him?

1. Explain the responsibility check.
2. Why are some customers challenging to one individual and not to another?
3. List and explain five characteristics of challenging customers.
4. What type of customer do you find to be the most challenging and why?
5. What are some methods of response to an angry customer who becomes verbally abusive?
6. How can you end discussions with overly talkative customers without offending them?
7. Contrast empathy and sympathy. Which is more productive?
8. Share a situation where you gave a customer incorrect information and then corrected your mistake.
9. Why is it important to end every customer interaction on a positive note?
10. What are some of the payoffs of coping with challenging customers?

MOTIVATION

REMEMBER THIS

The reward of a job well done is to have done it.

RALPH WALDO EMERSON

WHAT IS MOTIVATION? Every professional is at one time or another faced with the challenge of finding the motivation to perform a task or to fulfill an obligation. *Motivation is the individual drive that causes us to behave in a particular way.* Motivation is very personal. Different people are motivated by different rewards, experiences, and circumstances. The motivating force that causes one individual to get up every morning would not necessarily be enough to get their next-door neighbor out of their bed. It is because of the personal nature of motivation that managers, co-workers, and individuals are continuously seeking to develop a better understanding of what is necessary to create motivation. Motivation is important in both our personal and professional lives. Motivation may be the push that gets us started, or the gasoline that keeps us going.

Employees who work together will have differing levels of motivation at any given time. This suggests that co-workers will not all be involved in the same set of circumstances and may have more or less desire to accomplish a task or to work more quickly. An employee who will be starting a week's vacation as soon as work is completed may be especially motivated to complete the work. His or her co-workers, who do not have a vacation to look forward to, may be less motivated to work hard. When motivation levels vary it is helpful to work within a group. In this instance the possibility exists that when one employee is less motivated, others will be more motivated. Unfortunately, this is frequently not the case. This may result in one or more employees performing the bulk of the work while the others reap the benefits. This circumstance can greatly reduce motivation over time.

Ideally, motivation in customer service should flow from management to employee. Several methods of encouragement can be implemented to keep the enthusiasm of the customer service providers high. Recognition programs, suggestion rewards, and daily encouragement all help to keep customer service providers feeling good about the role they are playing in the overall provision of excellent customer service.

Some organizations create unique strategies to motivate their employees. Humor has been found to be an important part of today's motivated workplace. Individual companies approach the use of humor in different ways, but in most instances it can lighten a possibly stressful environment. Studies have shown that laughter can be the key to increased morale and overall job satisfaction. Humorous job titles, jokes of the day that come up on the screen when the computer is turned on, and theme dress days can all assist in adding humor to the professional workplace.

Other companies offer their employees the opportunity to participate in snack days when all employees bring their favorite "munchies," casual dress days, the opportunity to participate on the company softball team, to sit in company seats at a basketball game or symphony concert, annual company activities, monthly birthday celebrations, and numerous other creative motivational activities. The motivating force behind these activities is that they all enhance the unity of the employees. They create shared experiences that can bond employees. Employees who see themselves as an important part of a team are likely to feel a stronger sense of motivation.

Unfortunately, this type of positive leadership is not always available. It is in those situations that customer service providers must take responsibility for their own motivation.

NEEDS AND WANTS When attempting to understand the diversities of motivation, it is helpful to define needs and wants. *Needs are our personal requirements.* Some needs are instinctive, like the need for air and food; these are primary needs. Other needs are learned, like the specific foods that we enjoy or do not care for; these needs are called secondary needs. Both primary and secondary needs are vital to motivation. Many individuals have difficulty in viewing their real needs and may confuse them with wants. Most adults need some form of transportation to enable them to get to work and to fulfill their obligations. They *need* a basic automobile or access to public transportation, but in response to their needs they may *want* a sleek new car.

Wants are things or experiences that are desired. Wants have little relationship to needs. While the satisfaction of our needs satisfies our personal requirements, wants have little or nothing to do with what we must have. Individuals commonly desire what they do not really need. While this fact helps to drive the American economy, it may set some individuals up for disappointment, if they are unable to obtain what they perceive as their needs. Needs and wants are extremely motivational. Most individuals are willing to work hard to get what they want or need. Wants are frequently related to our self-image and reflect a desire to show others a visible display of our success or perceived success. A salesperson who is having difficulty in making his or her commission may, upon receiving a large check, purchase an expensive watch. In this instance, the salesperson's need to show himself and others that he is successful may overshadow his need to pay his rent.

When applying an understanding of needs and wants to motivation in a professional environment, misconceptions are common. What management perceives as being the needs of the employees may in reality have little importance and may have little motivational effect. An employee who has a day off coming, but who must work overtime so that he or she can take it, may perceive little or no motivational value from the day off. As frequently happens when attempting to understand expectations and perceptions, incorrect analysis may be made.

MOTIVATING FACTORS People have been trying to understand motivation for many years. Numerous studies have been conducted in the attempt to fully understand what motivates individuals. Motivation can be both positive and negative. A positive motivation would drive a travel agent to book enough vacations to qualify for a free trip. A negative motivation might drive an individual who is focused on losing weight to starve him- or herself. In both cases, motivation exists. It appears that the motivation to win the trip is of a more positive nature.

Some common motivating factors that have been discovered among adults are:

- Individual respect
- Challenging work
- Encouragement from management
- Financial security
- Opportunities to express creativity
- Job security
- Opportunities for advancement
- Unified work environment
- Good benefits
- A project approaching completion
- An approaching vacation
- Recognition from others
- Positive relationship with customers

While not all adults may be motivated by all of the above circumstances, many will find them to be driving forces that help them to stay focused and to accomplish their goals. Individuals must become familiar with their individual motivating factors. Frequently, employers fail to recognize the diversity of the factors that may motivate their employees. They may focus too much attention on the motivation realized from the employees' paychecks. When the company is unable to increase the employees' pay levels, the employer may perceive that the motivation is gone. Studies have shown that many adults believe that as long as their basic needs are being covered by their income, they will realize more motivation from other factors than just their paycheck.

Recognition is another motivating factor that may be misunderstood. A manufacturing company developed a program of recognizing outstanding employees by honoring them with a special luncheon and a commemorative mug. While the employees were honored to receive the special recognition, they were disappointed to find that the company made no special announcements to the other employees that the special employees had been honored. The only way for the honored employees' peers to hear about the honor was for the outstanding employees to spread the word themselves. This diminished the motivation that resulted from the honor.

UNDERSTANDING OF MORALE   *Morale is an individual's or group's feelings or attitudes toward a job, supervisor, or company.* High morale may result when employees are feeling good about their work, a high level of overall satisfaction is occurring, and employees are secure in their jobs. During high morale, employee loyalty and dedication are strong. High morale may be created by supportive management, a unified work environment, and individual, department, or corporate successes. High morale may result in increased productivity. Because employees are feeling good about their situation, they are less likely to miss work and are more likely to make an appropriate contribution while they are there.

Low morale exists when employees, and possibly management, are feeling less positive about their work and organization. Low morale may be caused by poor management, negative employees sharing their dissatisfaction with others, a company's uncertain future, rumored layoffs, too much work or overtime, and less than expected salary increases. Low morale can result in absenteeism, unprofessional behavior, and high turnover. Low morale may be difficult to correct. Even managers who are aware that it exists may have difficulty in changing it.

A company that announces on the television news that they will be laying off a number of their employees within the next several months will probably see a decline in employee morale. If an employee is uncertain about the employment future, he or she may find it difficult to have a positive feeling toward the organization and everyone associated with it.

SELF-CONCEPT AND MOTIVATION

Self-concept and motivation are linked in the process of enabling individuals to work productively with others. *Self-concept is the way in which a person sees himself or herself and thinks that others see him or her.* Individuals with strong self-concepts are able to view their own abilities in a positive way. They do not have to turn to others for affirmation; they find affirmation within themselves. A positive self-concept results in a person with the self-confidence necessary to deal with others in a professional and productive manner. Customer service providers must work to develop a positive self-concept. Angry customers may take out their frustrations on the person who is trying to assist them in finding resolutions to their problems. When this happens, it would be easy for an individual with a poor self-concept to take the customer's words or actions personally. A positive self-concept creates the armor necessary to keep customers' actions in perspective.

Unfortunately, many people do not have a positive self-concept. Society places a number of unrealistic examples of perfection before us. The media shows us that in order to be truly happy we must be attractive, tall, thin, witty, affluent, and perfect in every way. This example sets many people up for disappointment. How can we interact with the world in a positive manner if we are less than what we see as ideal? This is a challenge that faces most Americans.

Others are not influenced by the example that the media has established, but have been surrounded by negative people. Negative people can easily chip away at an individual's self-concept. If someone tells me that I am not good, why shouldn't I believe him or her? The most important thing that someone with a less than positive self-concept can do is to realize that he alone has the power to change the way he sees himself.

Individuals have the ability to improve their own self-concepts. While others can affect how individuals see themselves, change must begin within the individual. The first step in improving oneself is to perform a self-assessment. *A self-assessment is an individual evaluation in which individual strengths and weaknesses are identified.* A self-assessment helps individuals to determine where they are headed if they make no changes in themselves or in their behavior. A self-assessment must be performed honestly and is meant to evaluate the individual. Instances in which an individual believes that they have been overlooked or have experienced "bad luck" are not relevant during a self-assessment. Excuses and blame do not contribute to the performance of an accurate self-assessment.

To begin performing a self-assessment ask yourself the following questions and record your answers on a sheet of paper or on your computer.

1. **What are my strengths?** What do I receive compliments from others for having done well? What do I think that I am good at?
2. **What are my weaknesses?** What activities do I feel less confident in performing? Do I frequently make excuses or blame others for my failures? Do I finish what I start? Do I say yes too often? Do I pull my weight in a group activity?
3. **How do I see myself?** Am I dependable? Do I speak well in front of others? How is my sense of humor? What do I like most about myself? What do I like least? If I could change one thing about myself, what would it be?
4. **What are my likes and dislikes?** What kind of activities do I enjoy participating in? Do I like to sit in one place as I work, or do I like to move around? What subject did I enjoy the most while attending high school or college?
5. **Do I establish goals and work toward achieving them?** Do I take pride in successfully accomplishing a task?

It is not enough to perform a self-assessment. After you assess yourself, evaluate the information that you have recorded. When evaluating, it is helpful to draw conclusions and to develop a plan for the future. Review the responses that you recorded as you performed your own self-assessment. Are there specific areas in which you are pleased with your responses? As you draw conclusions about your strengths and weaknesses, recognize that the future will be much more productive if you consider your strengths and weaknesses as you establish goals.

Even if you were not entirely pleased with the outcome of your self-appraisal, you now have valuable new information about yourself. Most people have very little self-awareness because it is sometimes difficult to recognize who we are and how others see us. It is much easier to make excuses for our failures and to blame our circumstances on someone else. Do not dwell on any negative information that your self-appraisal may have revealed. Go forward making goals to emphasize the positive aspects of yourself and exploring ways to improve those areas that are in need of improvement. Above all, accept yourself as the unique person that you are.

Ten Tips for Improving Self-Concept

When working on improving your self-concept, try the following 10 tips:

1. **See yourself as a success**. Every individual has a special contribution to make to society. Those individuals who see themselves as successful will demonstrate more self-confidence as they interact with others. Seeing yourself as successful affects your actions. You will in most cases behave as a successful person because in your mind you see yourself that way. By dressing the part of a successful person, you will also demonstrate to others that you pay attention to detail. A person who presents a sloppy or extreme outward appearance may send the message to others that he or she lacks credibility or is not able to fit in well with others.

2. **Spend time with positive people**. Positive people tend to share encouragement with those that they spend time with. By surrounding yourself with positive people, you will be more likely to hear positive comments and to think in a more positive manner. Positive people see what can happen, not what can't. An individual who looks at the bright side of life will remind us of our successes at times when we are having difficulty seeing them.

3. **Eat right.** One of the challenges of leading a busy life is the temptation not to eat the foods that will make us healthy. It is easy to become so involved in carrying out our responsibilities that we neglect our own health. If location or time constraints require that you eat frequently at fast food restaurants, make the healthiest choices possible. Too much caffeine, from coffee, soda, or candy bars, can cause the body to experience high and low feelings. Try to drink six to eight glasses of water each day. Water will keep your body hydrated and will help you to avoid the highs and lows that frequently result from too much caffeine. If the temptation to hit the snack machine at break time is too great, plan ahead by bringing nutritious snacks from home. Carrot and celery sticks, raisins, fruit, or fat-free crackers can help to keep you going until your next meal.

4. **Break a task down into smaller steps.** Sometimes it is difficult to dive into a project because it seems overwhelming. A good way to

get started is to break the task down into several smaller tasks. If a quarterly report must be written, begin by creating the cover page. Then create the outline. Make the completion of the report a priority, but complete it a piece at a time. It also helps to become more organized. Make sure that your desktop, information system, paperwork, and message system are all organized so that you can operate at peak efficiency and follow through on the commitments that you make.

5. **Get enough sleep**. The average adult needs an average of eight hours of sleep per night. Try to determine the appropriate amount of sleep for you. If you awaken feeling tired, must always be awakened by an alarm clock, and tend to drag as the day goes on, you probably need more sleep. Try going to bed 30 minutes earlier each night for one week. If you are still tired, go to bed 45 minutes before your usual bedtime. By experimenting with different amounts of sleep, you should be able to recognize how much sleep your body really needs. Busy lifestyles may make it difficult to maintain a consistent sleeping schedule, but the benefits are worth it. A well-rested person usually has more patience, has a greater attention span, and is often more productive than someone who is tired. Feeling rested may help your self-concept to soar!

6. **Reward successes**. When you accomplish something that you are proud of, reward yourself! Most of us know when we have done a good job, but all too often we may forget to give ourselves a well-deserved pat on the back. Take yourself (and a friend) to lunch to celebrate, spend some time doing something that you enjoy, or smile with the satisfaction that you did something well. Some people find it helpful to keep a record of their accomplishments. This record can be a special file or list. Too many people focus on what they cannot do instead of what they can do. By acknowledging and rewarding our successes, we can recognize what we are good at and will have a sense of accomplishment.

7. **Practice positive self-talk**. Everyone talks to themselves occasionally. Unfortunately, what we say to ourselves is not always positive. By saying negative things to ourselves, whether out loud or silently, we reinforce negative thoughts and ideas. We may also begin to rehearse confrontations that we fear may occur. This may cause us to doubt our abilities and to focus too much attention on negative issues. Try talking positively to yourself. Talk out loud in your car or home and silently when around others. Tell yourself that you can handle the challenges that are placed before you. Be your own encourager! You can accomplish great things when you tell yourself, "You can do it!"

8. **Do something for someone else**. Doing something for someone else is often the best thing that we can do for ourselves. By helping someone else, we focus our attention on someone else's needs. Unselfishness has long been recognized as a boost to an individual's self-concept. Offer to help the new employee to learn the ropes, hold the door open for someone, take a sick friend dinner, walk your vacationing neighbor's dog, or do that little something extra for a customer. Everything that you do for someone else gives you an internal reward. You feel good about having done something. Whether or not the act is ever repaid is unimportant. You did it, that is what counts!

9. **Exercise!** More and more companies are recognizing the benefits of having fit employees. Even if your company does not have a wellness program in place, you can create your own individual fitness routine. When you exercise, the positive results include having more energy, fewer aches and pains, and valuable reflection time. Healthy employees tend to miss work less often and frequently approach challenges with a more positive attitude. Fitness counselors recommend that you always consult your doctor before embarking on a new fitness regimen. Finding the time to work exercise into your life may be challenging, but even a few minutes of stretching can be beneficial. A common time for exercise for professionals is in the morning. Fewer interruptions take away the opportunity for exercise if the day has just begun. To begin incorporating exercise into your daily life, try walking instead of driving (if that is reasonable), take the stairs instead of the elevator, do stretching exercises at your desk, or take a nice walk with a friend or loved one after work. The exercise will help you to feel better both physically and emotionally.

10. **Learn something new**. It is never too late to learn something new. A new trend among adults is to embrace the idea of lifelong learning. Lifelong learning means that we never assume that we know all of the answers or that we are too old to appreciate new ideas. Rapid changes in technology increase the need for additional training. In addition to gaining new knowledge, learning something new allows us the opportunity to meet new people, explore new ideas, and add new skills to our resume. To begin to discover the learning opportunities around you, read professional publications, learn new software programs, enroll in classes at the local community college, pursue an advanced degree, listen to books on tape, or devote time to learning something that you have always wanted to know how to do. Even if your learning does not apply to your professional position, you are broadening your knowledge

base and that will translate into new confidence that you will take to work every day.

POWER OF SELF-MOTIVATION

Customer service is frequently a thankless job. Unfortunately, our customers usually come to us when they have problems or are upset. To achieve excellence in customer service you must have the ability to review a situation and to motivate yourself. Behaviorists have studied motivation for many years and some of their basic conclusions have a few key commonalties. The most obvious one is that we all have motivations that cause us to do what we do. It is commonly suggested that we individually have the ability to motivate ourselves. This is sometimes the only motivation that we are going to get.

So how do individuals begin to motivate themselves? The following seven steps may provide a good start.

1. Post quotations that you find motivating at your workstation so that they can be seen throughout your day. If you surround yourself with positive messages, even the most challenging customer will have a hard time breaking your spirit.
2. Follow the tips for improving self-concept. By developing a strong self-concept, you will feel good about yourself, inside and out.
3. Set goals and strive to achieve them. By staying focused on your goals you will be more likely to accomplish them and to have the satisfaction of achievement.
4. Read motivational books or listen to motivational books on tape. Look for opportunities to listen while driving, taking a walk, or working out. The motivational message will stay with you after the tape is over.
5. If you are having a low energy day, walk, talk, and act like you are full of energy. Before long you will forget that you were tired and will feel as good as you look!
6. Develop your sense of humor and let others see it. A good laugh can help both you and those around you to feel refreshed and motivated!
7. Have fun! Motivated people accomplish their goals, feel good about who they are, and enjoy life.

By following the above steps for self-motivation you will embark on the positive journey to becoming and staying a motivated person. Serve as a motivator to others and they will in turn serve as motivators for you.

TEAMWORK

A recent *USA Today* article suggested that employees prefer working in teams to handling projects alone. *Teamwork is working together to improve the efficiency of the whole.* The idea of teamwork for many employees is appealing because employees can experience a unified approach to projects or work that does not exist when all responsibility rests with one individual. Some of the reasons that employees prefer teamwork according to a survey conducted for Dale Carnegie & Associates are:

- Indicated lower stress—72 percent
- Increased work quality—74 percent
- Improved attitude—67 percent
- Increased profitability—67 percent
- Increased productivity—66 percent

Teamwork does not work in every environment, but in those where it is appropriate, it can improve morale and result in a more positive and motivational work experience.

METHODS OF SAYING THANK YOU AND MOTIVATING OTHERS

Sometimes the most motivating action that we can share with others is to express our appreciation to them. Saying thank you does not have to be expensive, but it can have rewards that are beyond measure. While some companies do not recognize the benefits of expressing appreciation, many of the managers and companies that employees want to work for appreciate the tremendous power of recognition.

People need to see that their efforts are appreciated. Letting employees know that they have done a good job or that their extra attention in completing a project was noticed can be the motivating force that encourages them to keep up the good work. Many companies do not have the financial resources to allow, or may have trouble justifying the expense, of a monetary reward. Employees usually do not care how much a thank you costs, but will appreciate the recognition it implies.

Some inexpensive, but meaningful ways to say thank you are:

- Extend the lunch hour by 15 minutes.
- Bring donuts for the entire department to recognize an individual's or group's special efforts.
- Send a personal note of thanks.
- Give the employee corporate tickets to a special event.
- Acknowledge their contribution in a department or company newsletter.
- Designate a casual day in the employee's honor.
- Allow the special employee to leave work early to beat rush hour traffic.

Most employees will appreciate any recognition, no matter what it is. The motivating force behind the thank you is that employees and departments know that their efforts are noticed. Employees feel more pride in their work and in their contribution to the overall efforts of a company that is glad to have them as a part of the team.

SKILL BUILDING: HUMAN RELATIONS

The ability to interact effectively with and motivate others is an important skill to develop. By striving to improve human relations skills customer service providers prepare themselves for positive internal and external customer experiences.

Discuss and determine an appropriate resolution to the following human relations scenarios.

- Your company prefers that all employees adhere to policies when responding to customer requests. A few months ago you waived the policy and gave a customer an extension on their account. Until today, you had forgotten about the incident. A different customer called to request an extension. When you denied the customer's request, citing the policy, the customer responded by saying that they knew that you had waived the policy for the other customer. How can you respond to this situation and keep both the customer and your company happy?
- Recently you have noticed a morale problem in your own department. Employees are arriving late to work, are taking a lot of personal calls during work hours, and are complaining about things that previously were not problems. Since you have no real authority, how can you assist in improving morale and in making your department a nicer place to work?
- Last week you answered a customer's question. The customer was not pleased with the answer, and he left angry. Today, it came to your attention that the answer that you gave the customer was not correct. In fact, the correct answer is in the customer's favor. How can you contact the customer and convey the correct answer while maintaining your own professionalism?

3

PREPARE A COMPANY NEWSLETTER

CHALLENGE OBJECTIVES

1. To personalize the student's understanding of customer service.
2. To provide an opportunity to actively illustrate an understanding of customer service.
3. To successfully present to the others the completed newsletter.

ASSIGNMENT

Prepare a company newsletter for the company of your choice. This newsletter should be creatively presented and should be filled with suggestions about how to improve the employees' customer service. Your newsletter should be a minimum of two pages and a maximum of four pages. Review the newsletters that you have received observing style, content, and layout techniques. Attempt to create a newsletter that you would be motivated to read.

PSENTATION

Present your company newsletter in letter quality form. Your newsletter should be typed (and illustrated if you choose). It should be creatively displayed to encourage reading. Your newsletter should include the following:

1. A recognizable logo (your own design or someone else's).
2. A newsletter name.
3. At least one article related to customer service.
4. Your name listed as the editor of the newsletter.

Happy creating!

Helpful hint: Try using a desktop publishing or word processing program with a newsletter wizard to begin learning to create a newsletter. This is a good way to learn the program and to produce a professional document easily.

1. How can the use of humor aid in the motivation of employees?
2. What is the difference between needs and wants?
3. List some of your own needs and wants. Which needs and wants do you find the most motivating?
4. What are some of the motivating factors found to be common among adults?
5. Which motivating factors are most important to you individually?
6. What factors can cause low morale?
7. Why do you think that so many people have a poor self-concept?
8. Perform your own self-assessment.
9. How can a healthy diet enhance an individual's self-concept?
10. What can be done to increase self-motivation?

CHAPTER 9

LEADERSHIP IN CUSTOMER SERVICE

- LEADERSHIP DEFINED
- KNOWLEDGE OF YOURSELF
- FORMAL AND INFORMAL LEADERS
- COACH OR COUNSELOR
- CHARACTERISTICS OF EXCELLENT LEADERS
- LEADERSHIP AND GOALS
- CREATION OF A CUSTOMER SERVICE CULTURE
- BENEFITS OF JOB AIDS
- LEADERSHIP WITHOUT POSITION
- YOUR BOSS IS YOUR CUSTOMER TOO!
- SKILL BUILDING: LEADERSHIP
- OPPORTUNITIES FOR CRITICAL THINKING

REMEMBER THIS
The most valuable gift you can give another is a good example.

LEADERSHIP DEFINED

The customer service industry is in great need of leadership. *Leadership is the ability to influence others.* The most recognizably outstanding companies are known for their excellent leadership. Excellent leadership is a requirement of any business that provides products or services to customers. Leadership is not the automatic result of a title; it requires the development of effective leadership skills and practice in implementing them. Leadership skills are developed through the dedicated effort of individuals to improve their own abilities and to blend their own philosophies with those of their organization.

No company can produce outstanding service unless the key managers are obviously committed to and have a positive customer service philosophy. Rules and policies are not the answer. Policies promote consistency, but they are not capable of influencing others in a positive way; when presented improperly, they may appear harsh and unfriendly. Leaders have a vision of what can be and they share that vision with others around them. Excellent leaders serve as coaches, counselors, and positive examples. They have the skills to actually perform the work for which those they are leading are responsible.

Leaders must promote an interdependent environment. An interdependent environment constantly reminds employees that no one individual is responsible for an organization's success. Success comes as the result of the unified efforts of all participants contributing to the whole. The idea of interdependency means that no one individual should have to carry all the responsibility, with others reaping the benefits but not pulling their own weight. This philosophy is not instinctive. It must be created and perpetuated by the leaders of an organization. Anything less than an interdependent philosophy can breed a "that's not my job" mentality. When the leaders of an organization allow this mentality to set in, unity begins to fade away and disappears quickly.

Leaders demonstrate empowerment. They allow their employees to make a range of decisions to assist their customers. Excellent leaders train their employees to make decisions, which benefit both the customers and the company. Employees have confidence in their own abilities and are able to share enthusiasm and knowledge with customers without fear of making mistakes. By demonstrating interdependency, a vision for the future, and empowerment, excellent leaders create a culture in which excellence in customer service is the standard.

Customer service providers must serve as leaders for their customers. Through their interactions they share information, character, values, and enthusiasm with customers. Customers need leadership just as much as employees do. Customers feel more comfortable with products and services, methods of billing, the sharing of special circumstances, and special needs if they are treated with respect by an individual who is capable of leading them through the process to the next necessary step. Customer service providers have a tremendous amount of influence over their customers. All individuals in an organization must work to develop their own leadership skills so that they can be as effective as possible in their roles as leaders.

KNOWLEDGE OF YOURSELF

Leadership begins in our own minds. We must first see ourselves as leaders and then others will begin to see our leadership abilities. Leadership necessitates self-knowledge. Individuals must become aware of their own strengths and weaknesses. After identifying strengths and weaknesses, customer service providers can begin to overcome their weaknesses and to refine their strengths. A self-appraisal can be performed simply. By writing down strengths and weaknesses, customer service providers can determine a starting point.

To know yourself as a leader, ask yourself the following questions:

- How effectively do I relate to others?
- Do I practice excellent time management?
- What are my values?
- Is my knowledge level what it should be?
- Do I share my knowledge with others?
- Are my customers a priority to me?
- Am I willing to take risks?
- Do I establish measurable goals for myself?
- Do I willingly work toward department and company goals?
- Do I play mind games with my co-workers and superiors?
- Do I allow negative thoughts to cloud my attitude?
- Do I actively acknowledge accomplishments of others?
- Am I likeable?
- Do I willingly go above and beyond the call of duty?

These are not the only questions that will help customer service providers begin to develop self-knowledge of their leadership skills, but these questions are a good place to start.

No one can change someone else. People may try, but, in reality, change must begin from within. A manager has the following motto hanging on the wall of his department: "I am responsible for my own success, no excuses!"

This motto represents the manager's attitude toward the responsibility of his or her employees to change themselves. The business world today is highly competitive. Fewer and fewer people are getting ahead because of who they know. Advancement is more commonly based on an individual's proven abilities and desire to perform. Excuses do nothing but hold people back. Most of all, customers do not want to hear a customer service provider's excuses. Customers have enough of their own challenges. They want to interact with enthusiastic and well-trained customer service providers who can solve their problems.

Excellent leaders are self-confident. If others criticize them, they are willing to examine the area of criticism and determine if the criticism is deserved. If it is, they make changes and grow stronger from the experience. People want to be around self-confident people. Those with self-confidence have found approval within themselves, so they are not seeking it from others.

FORMAL AND INFORMAL LEADERS

Within any organization there exist several types of leaders. A common method of defining leaders is to categorize them as either formal leaders or informal leaders. *Formal leaders have the authority and power of their official position.* Formal leaders have been chosen by their organization to lead others. They may have been given special training to better prepare them for their roles as leaders. Formal leaders have a high level of accountability. Because the organization has selected formal leaders and has given them specific responsibilities, they are accountable to their superiors.

Informal leaders have no official authority, but do have the ability to influence others. Informal leaders are not chosen by management to fulfill their roles as leaders. The people who interact with informal leaders have unofficially appointed them. Frequently, informal leadership is an assumed role. Either an individual has unofficially taken on the role of leader, or others in a department, organization, or company have begun to think of and treat him or her as a leader. Informal leaders can either help or hurt the formal leadership of an organization. Informal leaders who do not support the goals of an organization or manager can undermine the efforts of the formal leadership. In this instance, they might use their influence to persuade other employees to be uncooperative or difficult. On the other hand, informal leaders who are supportive of the formal leadership and its goals can serve as motivating forces to encourage other employees to work together.

Both formal and informal leaders can contribute to the success of a customer service program. Formal leaders can create a culture that encourages excellent customer service. They can empower employees to make appropriate decisions and to serve as positive examples of what the company desires from employee performance. Informal leaders can also help to create a customer friendly culture. In addition, they can motivate their co-workers to higher levels of professionalism, can improve morale, and can relate to co-workers in areas where formal leaders may have difficulty.

The employees of a large utility company were experiencing a new philosophy in the way that management wanted them to approach their business. The leadership of the organization had always demonstrated the idea that their company was the only utility provider; therefore, the customers had to do business with them. This philosophy had resulted in a group of unmotivated employees who reluctantly came to work, dressed sloppily; who complained about how unappreciated they were; and who basically thought of customers as a huge inconvenience. When technology allowed new competition to enter the marketplace, the management of the company had to change its philosophy on the level of customer service which they were willing to provide. Suddenly, the same managers who were casually approaching every aspect of their business were telling their employees about the importance of customer service. The employees were not interested in changing their behavior. They resisted change and envisioned retirement on the horizon. It seemed that no matter what the formal leadership of the company did, it fell on deaf ears.

Out of desperation, they turned to the informal leaders whom they recognized among their employees. They did have a few employees who had positive attitudes, were excited about the new competitive approach to business, and who were highly influential with the other employees. These employees were invited to participate in updated customer service training and were encouraged to enroll in business courses at the local junior college. The employees were asked to help win over their co-workers—not in an obvious way, but through their actions. While this approach did not have immediate results, over a period of time it did prove to be effective. It became accepted behavior to come to work professionally dressed and with a professional attitude. The management of the company firmly believed that had it not been for the influence of the company's informal leaders, they would not have seen such a quick transition in attitudes and behavior of their employees.

COACH OR COUNSELOR Leaders serve as both coaches and counselors as they lead their employees. They must be available to train, correct, and encourage their employees. In addition they must help employees work through the challenges that may prohibit them from doing their best work. We are exposed to leaders early in life. The earliest leaders in a child's life are his or her parents, teachers, and coaches. It is from that early exposure that many future leadership expectations develop.

Employees need excellent leaders. They need to have someone who will consistently show encouragement, and who will help them to become successful. Good leaders have high expectations and their employees want to do things well. Excellent leaders recognize that employees want to be noticed. They observe employees' efforts and notice when they are successful and when they are experiencing difficulty. Leaders know that sometimes employees gain more from experiencing failure than from always experiencing easy success.

As coaches, leaders recognize the value of delegation. *Delegation involves assigning responsibility, granting authority, and creating accountability.* To delegate a task to employees means that the employees know what they are supposed to do and are trained to do it. They are given the power to get it done. Finally, they are expected to do it. If they do not do it, they are confronted and required to give an explanation. Accountability is one of the hardest aspects of delegation and of leadership because many individuals find confrontation difficult. Confrontation does not have to be negative. It is simply an opportunity to obtain additional information and to remind an employee of what was expected.

Good leaders notice what is happening with their employees and in their business. They are aware when things are going well as often as they notice when things are not going well. They are quick to reward others with a compliment or another form of recognition. Leaders usually reap what they sow. If employees are treated well by their leaders, they will usually treat their leaders well in return.

As counselors, leaders are good listeners. They allow others to share situations and ideas. They do not interrupt. Openness to new ways of doing things is a welcome mat to new ideas and may cultivate creativity. When others share confidences, excellent leaders respect the privilege of the information and keep the knowledge to themselves. The unique combination of coaching and counseling allows a leader to assist others in achieving individual excellence.

CHARACTERISTICS OF EXCELLENT LEADERS

The characteristics that describe excellent leaders are varied. While everyone has his or her own definition of what it takes to be an outstanding leader, some characteristics are important to all definitions.
Excellent leaders:

1. Show care and respect.
2. Practice what they preach.
3. Have expertise in the area in which they are working.
4. Practice consistency.
5. Behave professionally.
6. Allow employees to do what they have been empowered to do.
7. Give support.
8. Demonstrate flexibility.
9. Make time for others.
10. Are personable.

Excellent leaders are not afraid to praise the work of others. If you ask many salespeople and customer service providers they will tell you that praise makes them feel confident and competent. Studies have shown that workers with only average ability had an increase in their quality of work after their manager began a concentrated program of praising their performance and of giving constructive feedback to them in an encouraging manner.

Author Joseph Klock of *Selling Power* magazine suggests the following guidelines for praising employees:

- Praise in public at every opportunity.
- Before you tell your people what you don't like about what they have been doing, tell them what you do like.
- Provide frequent feedback.

Not everyone who becomes a formal leader will demonstrate the characteristics that describe an excellent leader. These are the skills to be developed and refined to become an excellent leader. At different times, while interacting with different people, leaders discover that some characteristics may be easier to display than others. This is representative of the diversity of people and situations. An excellent leader will always strive to be the most effective leader possible.

LEADERSHIP AND GOALS Leadership requires finding the balance between what has to be done and who has to do it. This balance can be realized because of the establishment of well-defined goals. *A goal is an identified result to strive to accomplish.* Goals must be written down. Goals that are not recorded tend to become resolutions that are easily forgotten and are rarely accomplished. *Goal setting is the process of establishing goals and of evaluating their importance.* To effectively determine goals, one must identify what needs to be accomplished. Goals can be established for small challenges and for large challenges. To effectively record a goal, the following three steps should be followed:

1. **Write down the overall goal to be accomplished.** Goals should be as specific as possible.
2. **Identify how the goal may be accomplished.** What has to happen for the goal to be successfully completed?
3. **Include a date or time when the goal will be completed.** A deadline gives a timetable during which the goal is to be accomplished.

Just establishing goals is not sufficient. Goals must be constantly pursued so that they are accomplished. Some individuals find it helpful to record their goals on cards and to display them so that they are continually reminded of the goals that they are working to achieve. The establishment of goals can serve as a motivator. The reminder that a goal is close to being accomplished can be the driving force that encourages a department or individuals to continue their efforts.

When establishing goals, it is helpful to begin with the end in mind. By recognizing the desired end result, individuals may be reminded of what is to come if the goal is achieved. In addition, actions are more likely to stay on track and therefore will be more productive. Goals are important in our professional and personal lives. Professionals should be familiar with the goals that their company has established for the organization. Professionals should also establish their own sets of personal goals. Personal goals should encourage personal growth, financial goals, and career advancement.

Sometimes one individual's goals can serve as an inspiration to others. A junior college student had a hard time making his college classes a priority; he enjoyed working and had a number of hobbies that distracted him from his studies. To help himself to stay on track and to accomplish the grades that he desired, he began establishing semester goals. His goals began small. The first semester his goal was to stay enrolled in all of his classes for the entire semester. He successfully accomplished his goal, but his grades were not very good. The next semester his goal was to stay enrolled in his classes all semester and to finish his classes with a grade of C or better. He again accomplished his goal. He began to see that he was succeeding in areas where he had not been successful previously. From this time forward, he established goals for each semester. One semester during a class discussion on goal setting, he shared his method of setting semester goals with the members of his class. The other classmates were inspired by his accomplishments. They were also inspired by his reward system. Every time that this student accomplished a goal, he treated himself to an activity in which he had long desired to participate. He decided on the reward at the same time that he established his goals. Because he had accomplished goals, he not only benefited from the original goal, but he had also gone hot-air ballooning, become certified in scuba diving, taken a hiking trip to the mountains, and the list went on! His reward system required that he also have a goal of having adequate finances available to pay for his reward, but that was a separate goal that he was motivated to accomplish. By the end of the semester, he had several other students who joined him as he celebrated his post-semester reward of hang gliding. They had also accomplished their semester goals! Today, this student is a successful real estate agent and he is continuing to accomplish his goals.

CREATION OF A CUSTOMER SERVICE CULTURE

Leadership in customer service is illustrated through the culture, which those in supervision create. As discussed previously, *culture consists of the values, beliefs, and norms shared by a group of people.* A customer service environment should have a customer service-oriented culture. If the "culture" does not encourage excellent customer service then excellent customer service will not happen. A part of the culture that the leadership of an organization can inspire is the attitude of the employees. Leaders can inspire positive attitudes even when the chips are down and things are not going as well as desired. This is when employees are really watching their leaders. If the leaders demonstrate that they are fearful of what is happening and suggest that they think that things are out of control, others around them will begin to feel the same way. Customer service requires much more than a positive attitude, but attitude is an integral part of the process.

If the culture requires that customers be treated with respect, the result will be, in most cases, that the customers will be treated with respect. This also requires that those in leadership roles live according to the rules of the culture. Too often, the leaders of an organization act as though they are the only ones who deserve respect. When this attitude and behavior is an accepted part of an organization's culture, little respect will exist.

Additionally, if the leadership provides a safe environment for taking risks, efficiency and creativity will probably be improved. A positive customer service culture should show respect and concern for employees, be helpful in assisting in the problem-solving process, and provide positive recognition whenever possible.

BENEFITS OF JOB AIDS   One of the common responsibilities of leaders is to provide training for their employees or co-workers. A well-trained workforce is one that is appropriately equipped to provide customers with excellent customer service. Unfortunately, one of the realities of training is that as time passes, some of the knowledge is forgotten. No one can remember every detail of training, especially if he or she did not have the opportunity to use the knowledge frequently.

Job aids can assist in circumventing this problem. *Job aids are leadership tools to reinforce training.* Job aids can take a number of forms. They can be anything from a concise how-to-operate card posted on the fax machine to a list of words to use placed at every customer service provider's work station. The important benefit of job aids is that they help people to do things correctly the first time. Job aids are usually a combination of visual information and written information. They should always be concise and to the point. Unfortunately, Americans have a documented aversion to instruction manuals. This makes the value of job aids even more important. The user may never have been taught or have read how to perform a procedure. A job aid can serve as a miniature training program.

Job aids are appropriate for both employees and for customers. Any situation in which a question may be asked concerning how to do something may indicate a need for a job aid. As technology continues to become a more important part of customers' lives, job aids will help them to actively take advantage of the technological opportunities. Job aids can remind users to use caution when operating dangerous equipment, and they can improve the safety of a work environment.

Many banks have added to their customer service offering by adding 24-hour automated account information lines. These telephone lines can provide customers with a considerable amount of information if the customers know how to operate them. If customers do not understand the operating procedure, they may get caught in a technological loop that will provide only frustration. To assist customers in using this technology, banks often send customers cards with the information line telephone number and with the specific numbers to press for the different types of account information. These cards can be posted near a telephone or can be carried in the customer's wallet for easy reference.

Job aids assist customers in being co-producers of their own customer service. Remember that co-production is when external or internal customers participate in providing at least a part of their own service. Job aids remind customers how easily they can do something. A large travel agency went to great expense to install a new telephone system. They invested additional money by providing extensive training for their employees so that they could use all of the features offered.

One month after the training was completed a check was performed to determine which of the features was being used the most. Unfortunately, the results were discouraging. Almost none of the new features were being used. In fact, very few employees had even recorded their own voice mail messages. The managers were called in and told to go back to their employees and to find out why the system was not being used. After the employees were surveyed it was discovered that although the employees were excited about all of the capabilities of the new telephone system, they could not remember how to perform all of the specific procedures. When the employees were working with customers all day, they did not have time to study the instruction manuals. After management became aware of the problem, they created job aids to be placed on all of the telephones explaining the main functions and procedures. Usage went up almost 100%! When the employees could easily reference how to use the system, they began using it.

Job aids are helpful in aiding the recall of all of the following:

- Computer command and software usage
- Recommended telephone greetings
- How to operate copy machines, fax machines, modems, or specialized equipment
- Steps in a problem-solving process
- Telephone system usage
- Safety precautions
- How to file insurance claims
- Anything else that employees or customers have been trained or encouraged to do

The creation of job aids requires a degree of creativity. Leaders must look for the opportunities in their own environment that could be enhanced by the addition of a supplementary leadership tool to reinforce training.

LEADERSHIP WITHOUT POSITION

Unfortunately, in customer service, management and staff sometimes have an adversarial relationship. Individuals who are supposed to act as leaders do not do so. In the area of customer service, all too often it is the managers who send their employees out to be trained in how to provide excellent customer service, while the managers lack the skills themselves. This can be discouraging for employees. In these instances it is necessary for informal leaders to take a leadership role. This means that employees who are respected by their peers and thought of as informal leaders can help to create an environment that encourages customer service, an environment which their managers may not be creating. This can be referred to as leadership without position.

Leadership without position may require a certain degree of assertiveness on the part of employees. Informal leaders or motivated employees can look for opportunities to share their leadership skills with others in an unofficial way. Any time that individuals interact in a positive manner an environment begins to become more unified. If employees want to have a more positive influence in their workplaces, they can be the ones to get it started.

Some things that you can do to show your leadership are:

1. Congratulate someone for handling a situation well.
2. Make suggestions to your supervisors of ways to help improve your efficiency.
3. Greet your co-workers with a smile.
4. Treat others as you would like to be treated.
5. Add your own positive method of showing leadership and encouragement.

YOUR BOSS IS YOUR CUSTOMER TOO!

One of the most challenging customers that you deal with each day may be your boss. Remember that your relationship with your internal customers is an important key to success in serving your external customers. Your relationship with your boss can make your professional life full of joy and reward or a daily dreaded task. Successful customer service providers are already actively attempting to understand and to meet the needs of their other customers, why not include your boss in that group?

To begin to meet and exceed your boss's expectations try the following:

- **Be a team player.** By allowing your boss to be the coach of his or her own team you give the boss the opportunity to lead you to accomplish organization or department goals.
- **Find out what your boss considers to be important.** By identifying your boss's priorities you develop an awareness of what he or she is striving to accomplish. You can then be of assistance in those specific areas.

- **Be a collaborator, not a complainer.** Nobody wants to be around someone who is always griping about something. If you disagree with how a project is being coordinated, share your ideas and take it in stride if your suggestions are not implemented. Never criticize, insult, or make fun of the boss to others. This is a reflection of your own bad attitude and others will recognize it. Being a part of the solution is much more positive than being a part of the problem.
- **Have reasonable expectations.** Your boss can only do what is within his or her power and ability to perform. In most work environments, several people report to their supervisor; therefore, you are not the only person they must consider when making changes or assignments.
- **Go to work each day with a great attitude and the willingness to be a professional.** Every individual must take responsibility for his or her own performance. Attitude plays an important role in how successful a person is in professional life. In addition, the willingness to embrace new technologies and systems may be challenging at first, but it will usually ignite a new enthusiasm for the customer, the work, and hopefully even the boss.

Through excellent leadership, the management and employees of companies can more effectively serve both internal and external customers and can demonstrate that they are accomplishing the goal of providing excellent customer service.

SKILL BUILDING: LEADERSHIP

Most individuals are in need of the positive influence that an excellent leader shares with those around them. Excellent leaders become positive examples for others because they have recognized and have worked to refine their interaction skills. By observing individuals who demonstrate positive leadership we can identify qualities to develop in ourselves.

Identify one individual who, in your opinion, is an excellent leader. List the qualities that this individual demonstrates as he or she interacts with others. Include such qualities as level of expertise, personality, etc.

Now, examine and list your own qualities as a leader. Even if you are not in a formal leadership role, you probably still possess leadership abilities. After listing your own leadership qualities, compare them to those of the excellent leader that you observed. Develop goals that can help you to enhance and improve your current abilities so that you can begin to become a more skilled leader.

OPPORTUNITIES FOR CRITICAL THINKING

1. Identify five qualities of a good leader.
2. List and explain four things that can be done to show leadership without position.
3. Why are many of the companies that are recognized for providing outstanding customer service known for their outstanding leadership?
4. Explain an interdependent environment. How important is it?
5. How seriously should an organization regard its informal leaders?
6. List some characteristics of excellent leaders.
7. Why are so many individuals in leadership such poor leaders?
8. Have you seen individuals who establish goals accomplishing them? Do you set your own goals?
9. What is a job aid? Create a job aid that would assist your internal or external customers.
10. What does leadership without position mean?

CUSTOMER RETENTION AND MEASUREMENT OF SATISFACTION

REMEMBER THIS
A truly satisfied customer shall return!!

UNKNOWN

WHAT IS CUSTOMER RETENTION? *Customer retention is the continuous attempt to satisfy and keep current customers actively involved in conducting business.* The importance of keeping current customers has been known for a long time. Interestingly, even though managers have recognized this fact, very few have created an active approach for keeping customers. Most businesses are focused on finding new customers, not on maintaining the existing customers. Numerous businesses send salespeople out to make the initial sale and then leave customer maintenance to the customer service department. The trend today is to recognize the importance of those customers who have already made the commitment to do business with us and to create an environment that encourages those customers to continue to work with us.

Most individuals who work with customers know that it is much more costly to attract new customers than it is to keep the ones that we already have. In spite of this knowledge, most companies do not have a plan specifically designed to maintain a relationship with existing customers. For many companies the plan is informal to the point of being nonexistent. Most customer service providers and salespeople know they should be nice to their customers, but it takes a more deliberate approach to retain customers. Some companies follow up with their customers when business is poor and they are in need of additional income. This is a poor representation of a customer retention program. A well-developed plan for customer retention creates an environment where current customers' needs are met on an ongoing basis and new needs are explored. Customers are reminded by their experiences that they are valued customers of a company and thus they wish to continue to do business with that company. Real customer retention consistently reminds customers that they are important. The result of customer retention is that customers will be so satisfied by a company that they are not motivated to seek other opportunities. They see that their dollars are well spent and that they are receiving a positive return on their investment. Customers also develop a stronger loyalty to those companies that show an interest in them.

VALUE OF EXISTING CUSTOMERS Existing customers have a tremendous value! They know how our company approaches business. Existing customers know us and our policies. They are familiar with our products and services. They frequently buy without requiring a sales pitch. They will not tolerate a decline in our quality, but they will consider new product or service offerings more easily.

Our existing internal customers are especially important. We must work to maintain our internal customer relationships. Internal customers are frequently taken for granted. Because internal customers are the people we work with, it is difficult and sometimes impossible to find new internal customers. Internal customers may not be able to stop doing business with us, but they can become difficult to work with. Anything that unifies internal customers can have a positive effect on the success of a business.

Existing customers want our company and us to expand our offerings. The more we can do for them, the easier it is for them to do business with us. All customers want to feel appreciated, even those cooperative customers who have never had a complaint. Unfortunately, it is easy to overlook the customers who are most important to us. A customer who has done business with a department store for a number of years and who has a store credit card may resent the store's offering new credit customers a special discount on their first purchase if they open a new account. The long-term customers may or may not have received special incentives when they opened their accounts, but, if time has passed, the appeal of the initial offering has been forgotten. The long-term customers want an up-to-date display of the company's appreciation for their business. What can the department store do? Discount coupons, preferred customer mailings, deferred billings, and invitations to special events can be positive incentives. With the competition that exists in business today, there is always another company working to attract our customers' business.

Customer retention is not dependent on technology. Technology may assist in the process, but customer retention is really nothing more than common courtesy, showing customers that you care for and appreciate them. A person once said: "Don't date your customers; marry them." What were they talking about? If we "marry" our customers, we make a commitment. We let them know that we are in an ongoing relationship. We do not just show our positive qualities and hope that our weaknesses never show up. By "marrying" our customers, we show them that we are concerned with their success and happiness today and in the future.

As companies enter into financial commitments, which is what doing business is, they are weighing the reasons why they should commit their dollars. They want to know that they are getting a "bang for their buck." If they are not, they may choose to allocate their dollars elsewhere. One area where the need for customer retention is especially important is in the area of non-profit business. Businesses that seek donations or time from individuals must have a customer retention program in place. Customers are becoming cautious about how and where they invest their money and time. If they do not see it going for a worthwhile cause or do not see that they are getting anything from the investment, they may redirect their spending. Few individuals would want to return to a social, civic, or religious organization that didn't periodically say thank you or acknowledge their presence until they were gone.

UNDER-STANDING CHURN

Marketing programs within established organizations, large and small, continue to focus on attracting new customers while the needs and desires of current customers are frequently neglected. What this approach fails to benefit from is the tremendous value of satisfying and retaining existing customers. A way to measure the significant value of retaining existing customers is to measure the Churn Rate, Defection Rate, and Customer Lifetime Value of customers for a given year. *Churn (or Churn Rate) is the number of customers who leave in a year's time divided by the number of new customers in the same period.*

Churn = (number of defections) divided by the (number of new customers)

This tells us that if 210 customers stop using a service and 350 customers purchase it for the first time, there is a *60%* churn rate.

Defection Rate is the percentage of your customers that leave you in one year.

Defection Rate = (customers left) divided by (customers had)

If we began the year with 1,000 customers and ended the year with 350 fewer accounts, our defection rate is 35%.

Customer Lifetime Value is the net present value of the profits a customer generates over the average customer life.

Customer Lifetime Value = (yearly profit) × (customer life in years)

If your average customer generates $2,000 in profit per year and your average customer life is 8.7 years, then your Customer Lifetime Value before factoring in net present value is $17,400. Once you know how much it costs to lose a customer, you can make decisions regarding investments to retain customers (Source: Bernard R. Cohen, *TeleTimes* magazine). From this method of determining churn, defection rate, and customer lifetime value it is easy to determine that even a small reduction in customer defections can result in positive profit results.

How to Tell if You Need to Improve Your Customer Retention Program

If you do not have answers for all of the following questions it is time to develop a customer retention program within your company.

1. Is customer satisfaction your primary management objective?
2. Is customer satisfaction measured and assessed regularly?
3. If there a constant effort to enhance customer satisfaction?
4. Do you measure quality standards and communicate results to your employees?
5. Do you train and retrain your customer service providers?
6. Do you have an employee turnover problem?
7. How much do you spend to keep current customers?
8. What is your current cost for acquiring a customer?
9. What is your average annual customer dollar value?
10. What is your current customer defection rate?
11. How do you get lost customers back?
12. Do you constantly deliver what you promise to your customers?

(Source: Bernard R. Cohen, *TeleTimes* magazine)

DEVELOPMENT OF A CUSTOMER RETENTION PROGRAM

When developing a customer retention program, it is important to create one that is manageable and that supports the goals of the organization. Some of the most basic approaches to customer retention are: Follow-up phone calls, face-to-face visits, special events, name recognition, reminder faxes, coupons, newsletters, and the willingness to do a little something extra.

Customer retention requires initiative. It means that customer service providers must tune in to what the customer needs and be ready to suggest new opportunities. It also means that providers must cultivate relationships with customers and convey the message that the customer is more than just a business contact.

One company began its customer retention program by implementing "Fun Fridays." One Friday of each month was designated as "Fun Friday." On "Fun Friday" every employee in the organization stopped what they were doing to call an assigned number of customers. The time allotted for calling was 10 minutes. The goal was to reach all customers by phone at least once a year. The customer conversations were opportunities to ask the customers how they were doing, if they had any special needs, and to let them know that their business was greatly appreciated. To add to the excitement of "Fun Fridays," employees were allowed to dress casually, were served donuts in the morning, and qualified for prizes by participating. Everyone from the president to the mailroom clerks participated in calling customers on "Fun Fridays." An additional benefit of "Fun Fridays" was that those employees who previously had not had the opportunity to interact with customers began to feel as though they too had customer relationships. By allowing everyone to participate, no one individual or department had all of the responsibility for customer retention.

When establishing a customer retention program, remember the following:

1. **Examine who your customers are and what specific needs they have.** If you understand who your customers are, a customer retention program can be effectively created to cater to them and their business needs in an appealing manner.
2. **Identify specific objectives to be realized by the program.** Determine what is to be accomplished by the creation of a retention program. Objectives should be specific: To increase sales, to improve communication, or to enhance customer loyalty.
3. **Create a manageable program of customer retention.** Customer retention programs should be manageable. They may need to start small and grow as they become successful and become a part of doing business.
4. **Create a culture that stimulates customer interest.** Management should provide an employee environment that makes it acceptable and appropriate to encourage customers to continue to do business

with their company. Management should also provide active examples of their philosophies in managers' behaviors.

5. **Determine a timetable for evaluation.** When a customer retention program is developed, it should designate a time at which an evaluation process will be implemented. At the time of evaluation, improvements can be made and successes can be recognized.

MEASUREMENT OF SATISFACTION

As we strive to provide customers with excellent customer service, we must periodically measure our customers' satisfaction. As discussed in Chapter 1, customer satisfaction is the customer's overall feeling of contentment with a customer interaction. When attempting to measure our customer's satisfaction, expectations and perceptions must be considered. To measure satisfaction, frequent questions must be asked of many customers. The most common method of asking questions to determine satisfaction are through the use of a survey. When creating a customer measurement device, it is important to ask relevant questions that will provide an opportunity to generate helpful information.

When creating a format for measuring customer satisfaction, ask

- who the customers are
- how they began doing business with your company
- where they are located
- where they conducted business with you (if there are multiple locations)
- when they did business
- what they liked about the experience
- in what way you could do a better job

To effectively measure customer satisfaction, we must look at the customers' situations from their perspectives. A measurement format should be to the point and should not take more than a couple of minutes to complete. If it must be returned by mail, it should have a postage paid indication. Most customers will not seek out postage to mail a customer response unless they are very upset with our performance.

A discount store conducted a survey to determine what the customers liked or did not like about the store. The survey asked questions about the interior lighting, ease of finding merchandise, prices, and many other questions that would help provide better service to the customers. They did not ask anything about the parking lot or how safe the customer felt coming in to the store. One customer responding to the survey had very positive responses to all of the questions about the interior of the store. When he or she was being thanked for participating in the survey, the customer asked if there were no questions to be asked about the parking lot. The survey administrator responded by saying that the parking lot was not important to the store at this time. This was not the right response for this customer! The customer shared that although there was satisfaction with everything inside the store, he or she was hesitant to come to the store after dark because of the inadequate lighting in the parking lot. There was also concern about the lack of identifiable handicapped parking spaces, the lack of lines dividing the parking spaces, and the number of stray shopping carts that could possibly damage surrounding cars. What this experience showed the company was that the original survey was not creating an accurate picture of how the customers felt about doing business with the company, and that although things inside the store met the customers' expectations, the customers might not come inside because of the parking situation.

SOURCES OF INFORMATION   There are several sources for obtaining information about customers' satisfaction. The following list includes some possible sources.

1. **Informal surveys**—Informal surveys can provide insights about what customers like and dislike. Informal surveys may not be statistically measurable, but they can help businesses to know their customers better.
2. **Comment cards**—The use of comment cards is one of the most popular methods of determining a customer's satisfaction. They are easy to create and are frequently available from company home offices. They do not provide detailed information, but they can provide immediate feedback. Customers may complete comment cards while they are involved in the customer experience.
3. **Verbal comments**—Verbal comments are easy to collect, but they are often ignored. By asking customers about their experiences, information can be obtained. To accurately collect information from verbal comments, employees must be encouraged to document comments on a customer log so that the comments are not lost.
4. **Historical data (point of sale)**—With the use of computers in most workplaces, it is easy to collect historical data. To find out how much customers have purchased, how often they have purchased, and other related data, the information can be accessed at the touch of a button. Unless it is incorrectly entered, historical data can be a very accurate resource for understanding customers. While historical data does not allow for emotion or opinions, it does give information concerning what is actually happening.
5. **Sales**—Like historical data, sales do not show emotion, but they do show what customers are currently doing. If they are increasing or decreasing orders, this will be reflected in sales. Sales are a current indication of customer satisfaction, but they should be used in combination with other sources of information.

6. **Corporate generated surveys**—Many corporations generate surveys that are sent to their customers. Corporate generated surveys are usually more detailed than informal surveys and the data that they reflect is usually statistically measurable. Corporate generated surveys may ask questions about products as well as the service that was received. Corporate generated surveys can collect a quantity of information, but they may have a lower response rate, depending on the customers surveyed.

7. **Discussions with internal customers**—Internal customers frequently have information about what customers like, don't like, and are interested in. If internal customers are never asked what their customers have told them, they may never have the opportunity to share their valuable information. Internal customers usually know what is not working well for customers and where snags in the system exist.

8. **Focus groups**—Focus groups are random groups of customers or prospective customers who are brought together to discuss current or future offerings of a business. Focus groups are sometimes challenging to coordinate, but they can cultivate a creative approach to understanding customers. Questions can be asked of the group and the responses can be recorded for future development.

9. **Toll-free phone numbers**—By providing our customers with toll-free numbers to reach our company or department easily, we can encourage them to contact us when a question or problem arises. Toll-free numbers should be answered promptly by knowledgeable employees who are well trained in answering customer questions and in responding to customer concerns. Some customers will call to share observations as they are occurring. These same customers might not take the time to convey their observations in writing. Customer comments should be documented so that they can be considered with other sources of customer information.

10. **Customer intelligence information**—Remember, *customer intelligence is the process of gathering information, building a historical database, and developing an understanding of current, potential, and lapsed customers.* The use of customer intelligence allows businesses to build on information already gathered and to add new information to get a total understanding of the unique customer relationship. By not having to rediscover information already gathered, problem identification and solving can begin more quickly and affordably.

BENEFITS OF MEASURING YOUR EFFECTIVENESS

Several benefits can be realized by measuring a company's or a department's effectiveness. By measuring effectiveness, weaknesses can be discovered so that corrections can be made. New customer needs can also be recognized so that new programs can be created and implemented to satisfy customers' current needs. Since customers may frequently not share ideas and problems unless they are asked, the creativity of customers may go unnoticed. According to the *Harvard Business Review* a 5 percent increase in customer retention yields about 25 percent to 125 percent increase in profits.

A wonderful benefit of measuring effectiveness is that we can discover what we are doing well. Customers are often quite satisfied by our offerings but unless they are allowed to share their satisfaction, the offering may be changed or updated to a degree that the customer may become dissatisfied.

TIPS FOR REALISTICALLY DETERMINING YOUR EFFECTIVENESS

When attempting to realistically determine effectiveness, it is important to ask well-developed questions. Those questions should be asked of a variety of customers so that responses reflect the spectrum of customers that are served. If a problem exists that is not going to be corrected, no matter what customer responses are, it should not be presented to customers for consideration.

Explain why the questions are being asked. Express advance appreciation to the customer before he or she shares information. Thank the customers for having taken valuable time to share their responses. Explain that through the responses of many customers, the company can attempt to improve its services and continue with services which are currently meeting the needs of customers.

WHY SURVEYS DON'T ALWAYS REFLECT REALITY

One of the most common methods of measuring customer satisfaction is through the use of surveys and comment cards. While these are the most common methods of measurement, they do not necessarily reflect a real picture of customer satisfaction. Frequently, the primary customers who take the initiative to respond to surveys and comment cards are those customers who are dissatisfied with their experience or those customers who hope to gain from their comments. Satisfied customers may not take the time to express their satisfaction and therefore may not be included in the overall picture of satisfaction.

An additional problem with surveys and comment cards that may make them unreliable sources of information is the method of questioning that is used. This may be reflected in both the way that the questions are asked and the specific questions that are asked. Information may come back as being very positive, when in reality there are problems. Questions can be asked so that they avoid subjects that may receive negative responses. If a company has areas of customer interaction that are known by employees as in need of improvements, but upper management is not aware of them or upper management is being shielded from the information, these are areas that may never be addressed. Questions can be worded in such a manner that the information will not be revealed.

Surveys may not ask enough questions to establish valid information. A survey was circulated to establish customer interest in a new service that would be available for customer use after hours. The survey asked if the customers would like to see the new service offered; it also asked if the customer would like to participate in using the service. The survey results were overwhelmingly positive. The service was added. Unfortunately, very few customers ever took advantage of the service. The company was perplexed about how the survey results could so overwhelmingly suggest that the service was desired and then have so few customers who were taking advantage of its offering. A second survey was circulated to the same customers; the only addition to the original survey was the question, "Would you actively participate in using this service?" The response was that almost none of the customers said yes. Upon further analysis, it was discovered that although the customers thought that the service sounded like a wonderful idea, most did not see that they would actually be able to use it. The omission of one question greatly affected the validity of the survey.

IDEAS FOR EVALUATING YOUR OWN PERFORMANCE

Sometimes the most effective method of evaluating customer satisfaction is to evaluate your own performance. If we examine the areas of our company and department that have the most questions asked, we may identify strengths and weaknesses without going to the customer. To evaluate your own performance ask yourself these questions:

- Do my customers know that I am here to assist them with any questions that may arise?
- Am I well informed about the systems that my company offers to customers?
- Do I convey enthusiasm and interest in my customers?
- What skills could I develop that would enable me to better assist my customers?
- Do I practice name recognition and work at developing a relationship with my customers?
- What else could I do to assist my customers and department as we work to provide excellent customer service?

WHAT MEASUREMENT OF SATISFACTION MEANS TO YOUR BUSINESS

By measuring our customers' satisfaction we deepen our relationship with our customers. We consider the customers' level of satisfaction, their expectations, and their perceptions. We ask questions and create an environment that encourages the sharing of ideas and concerns. The message that is conveyed to customers is that our company is interested in what they think and our company is also willing to actively strive to satisfy them. The seeking of feedback from customers can in itself result in positive customer retention.

SKILL BUILDING:
CUSTOMER RETENTION

The value of existing customers is greater than many organizations realize. Unfortunately, most organizations direct the majority of their customer efforts toward new customers and therefore do not effectively meet the needs of the customers they already have.

Customer retention is the continuous attempt to satisfy and keep current customers actively involved in conducting business. Customer retention efforts do not have to be expensive and are frequently not dependent on technology. The best customer retention programs start small and encourage communication while reminding the customer that the organization is still out there ready to serve them.

Either individually or in a small group, list 10 creative elements that would seek to keep current customers involved in your business. Your ideas should reflect the specific customers that you interact with and their own unique set of needs and circumstances.

1.

2.

3.

4.

5.

6.

7.

8.

9.

10.

After recording the creative elements that would seek to keep current customers involved, rank them according to how easy they would be to implement.

By exploring the customer retention ideas that you have recorded, you have established the basis for a customer retention program. Share your ideas with others in your organization and begin the process of retaining customers!

WRITE YOUR OWN PHILOSOPHY OF CUSTOMER SERVICE

There are as many different interpretations of customer service as there are individuals. In spite of the fact that business people and customers are talking about the importance of customer service, many have never defined for themselves, or for someone else, what they believe customer service to be. Customer service providers must combine the knowledge that they have acquired about customer service with the realities of their professional environment. This definition of customer service becomes your individual philosophy. A philosophy is the combination of the ideas and convictions of an individual. In customer service, a well-developed and realistic philosophy can be the key, not only to success in the industry, but also to differentiating between individuals when they are applying for employment or are candidates for advancement.

CHALLENGE OBJECTIVES

1. To allow students the opportunity to develop their own philosophy of customer service.
2. To integrate the students' up-to-date knowledge of customer service with their own experiences and day-to-day realities in the industry.
3. To convert ideas to words successfully and concisely.

ASSIGNMENT

Consider the knowledge that you have acquired about customer service. Combine this knowledge with the practical experiences that you have had in customer service situations (both as a customer and as a provider). Write, as concisely as possible, your philosophy of customer service. Your philosophy should include 1) how you define customer service, and 2) what you believe about customer service. Include any examples that you feel are pertinent and any other information that you feel supports your position.

PRESENTATION

Prepare your philosophy of customer service in written form. Remember, your philosophy of customer service is completely your own. You may include specific definitions and ideas that were discussed in the book, but it should also include other specifics as to why you believe what you do. Be concise.

1. List five sources of information that would give insights as to the quality of a business's customer service.
2. Define *customer retention*.
3. What is the one thing that you and your company could do to retain your current customers?
4. Why is maintaining existing customers so important?
5. How do you measure churn or churn rate and why is it an important number to know?
6. What are some guidelines to consider when creating a customer retention program?
7. Create your own device for measuring customer satisfaction. Try to limit it to 10 questions or fewer.
8. Verbal comments from customers are sometimes the easiest to get. Why are they not always the most accurate measure of customer satisfaction?
9. What are some questions that can assist an organization in evaluating its own performance?
10. Why should all customer service providers develop their own philosophy of customer service?

DELIVERING CUSTOMER SERVICE TO THE CHANGING MARKETPLACE

- TODAY'S CHANGING MARKETPLACE
- UNDERSTANDING THE CUSTOMER OF THE 21ST CENTURY
- EMBRACING NEW TECHNOLOGIES
- CALL CENTERS
- CUSTOMER SERVICE OVER THE INTERNET
- ENHANCING SERVICE EXPERIENCES AND BUILDING CUSTOMER LOYALTY
- SKILL BUILDING: TECHNOLOGY TRAINING
- OPPORTUNITIES FOR CRITICAL THINKING

REMEMBER THIS

The absolute fundamental aim is to make money out of satisfying customers.
SIR JOHN EGAN

TODAY'S CHANGING MARKETPLACE

Today's marketplace is changing rapidly. Opportunities that once seemed possible only in the distant future are now upon us. Customers are embracing these new opportunities with an enthusiasm that sometimes exceeds business' ability to deliver. In addition, customers may expect businesses to offer services that they are not quite ready to offer. This results in either offering services ahead of schedule or in not offering them and being perceived as behind the competition.

A chain of pizza restaurants with an enormously successful delivery system recently introduced their own website to handle orders, customers' comments, and complaints. This introduction was due to repeated customer request, although the company management was doubtful as to whether the website was needed, would prove profitable, and would enhance the already successful delivery business. Customers liked the novelty of logging on to complete one more transaction in their busy lives. The verdict is still out on the profitability of the new venture. More and more businesses are being faced with this kind of decision. Introduce a service that optimizes current technology prematurely or refrain from introducing it and appear behind the times.

UNDERSTANDING THE CUSTOMER OF THE 21ST CENTURY

Customers in the 21st century will be more sophisticated in the ways that they search for and make purchases. They will expect from service providers:

1. Availability: services designed to meet the customer's schedule
2. Accessibility: when the customer needs to talk, the provider can be reached
3. Accountability: customers prefer quick and accurate answers to service questions (Charlene Taylor: *Rural Telecommunications* magazine, Nov/Dec 1996)

Customers want hassle-free customer experiences that are user friendly and that validate the customer's choices. Customers want to feel that they are highly valued and that service responses are available when the customer *really* needs them. Customers have busy lives today and will continue to have them. It is unlikely that customers are installing software for home use or will need to ask lawnmower repair questions during the hours of 9 to 5 Monday through Friday. Finally, customers want to have service experiences that provide accurate answers in a timely manner. They also will expect increasing levels of accountability from the organizations they enter into business with. Surveying customers will not be enough to discover their preferences. Customers will expect the opportunity to offer their suggestions.

A new marketing strategy is being offered in several metropolitan areas, which promises "hassle-free" automobile purchases and accessible service and is described as "Car buying for the new millennium." When a customer recently called to make an appointment for an oil change, she was told that noon was not a good time to bring the car in because the oil change technician would be at lunch. When the customer expressed the need to take care of this errand during the lunch hour, she was told that perhaps *the customer* could take a late lunch! The customer then stated that she could take the car to the oil change specialist down the street and that the specialist was *never at lunch,* the price was *cheaper,* and that the car would be returned with the *windows washed* and the *interior vacuumed.* The customer did make an appointment and hung up. After thinking about her choice for awhile, she decided that she would take her car to the other company for the oil change. When she called the dealer back, out of courtesy, to cancel the appointment, the on-hold message spoke of how the company was created to serve the customer. After hearing the message several times and still being on hold, the customer hung up, frustrated and angry about how out of touch the company was with real customers. This is a perfect example of a company that is talking about service, but obviously does not have a clue as to the real needs of their customers. Customers no longer stand for this kind of treatment. They take their business elsewhere and then when the company feels the loss of customers they all too often blame the economy or state that there is too much competition for the limited customer base. Customers will expect enhanced service opportunities and will not settle for less than what meets their ever-changing needs.

EMBRACING NEW TECHNOLOGIES

Technology is progressing at a rate that is staggering. Customers are anxious to experiment with new technological options with the hope that they will be of benefit to them in some way. One possible reason that customers are more responsive to new technologies is that they have become, in many cases, very user friendly. As it becomes easier to understand and work with a system, people will be drawn into using it. The positive benefit of this trend is that the standard of excellence is raised and in most cases the speed at which business is conducted increases. Some of the most rapidly advancing technologies that customers are seeking out and using are customer service call centers, customer service over the Internet, and e-mail.

When new technologies are introduced in the workplace they are often greeted with a mixture of emotions—everything from enthusiasm to terror! New technologies mean new things to learn and old habits to break. To prepare others to greet the opportunities of new technologies with an open mind take the following steps:

- **Prepare your staff.** Get the call center staff involved from the start.
- **Train supervisors and team leaders first and get them to buy in.**
- **Develop a group of "change champions"** who will act as advocates for the new technology.
- **Sell your vision.** Convey your enthusiasm and share how much easier work will be.
- **Praise successful use of the new technology.**

- **Resist the temptation to complain.**
- **Celebrate small successes.** Celebrate small milestones along the way to keep all involved excited.
- **Avoid the "shelfware syndrome."** This is the temptation to give up and put the new technology on the shelf, never to be used. (Source: Dr. Jon Anton, *Customer Service Manager's Newsletter,* May 10, 1998)

CALL CENTERS   One of the most dramatic growths in customer service is service offered via the customer service call center. According to *U.S. Direct Marketing Today,* approximately 60,000 U.S.-based call centers exist today and the number is growing all of the time. Call centers have a unique advantage when delivering customer service. They can be located just about anywhere that has a sufficient worker base and one call center site may handle a number of different companies' calls. Customers are accepting a little less one-on-one service for increased convenience. Call centers allow service costs to be reduced from the costs resulting from face-to-face encounters.

Call centers now include the category of teleselling. Previously referred to as telemarketing, *teleservices is selling products, services, or information via the telephone.* Two types of calls fall within the area of teleservices. *Inbound calls are calls that originate with the customer that may include catalog ordering, billing questions, technical support, product use, or other information. Outbound calls are calls that originate from the call center to the customer, usually intended to sell products or services, conduct market research, or respond to customer inquiries.* Many call centers handle both inbound and outbound calls.

Most customer service call centers have sophisticated telephone systems that include special call routing features so that calls are routed to the next available service provider. They may be linked to a "call me" web browser feature that allows customers linked with a company's Internet site to be referred to a call center representative. The call center representative then calls the customer to respond to the customer request.

The call center workplace is a fast-paced environment focused on serving the customer as quickly and professionally as possible. The call center is not for everyone, but individuals with excellent telephone skills, ability to handle stress, good computer skills or the aptitude to learn new computer systems, ability to stay at their workstations, enthusiasm, positive attitude, motivation, good problem-solving skills, professionalism, and the ability to see a call through to the end would be excellent candidates for call center positions. Because of the importance of telephone skills, many candidates are interviewed by telephone to identify their telephone techniques.

CUSTOMER   The growth of the Internet has exceeded most of the experts' predictions.
SERVICE OVER   The importance of the Internet in the area of customer service is dramatic.
THE INTERNET   A report by Forrester Research Inc., a technology research firm in Cam-

bridge, Massachusetts, predicts that Internet customer service will cut the cost of labor per customer contact by 43 percent by the year 2000. So many customer services can be offered via the Internet that companies must attempt to identify whether or not a website would enhance their service offering. Product and company information, new products, ordering options, answers to commonly asked questions, owner's manuals, part reorders, and technical updates are some examples.

Call centers can provide considerable information and assistance to customers. A website can supplement what the call center is doing. Because so many consumers now have Internet access and actively use it, it makes sense that they would try a web search to gain information or assistance from a company before they would track down a 1-800 number. By offering information via the Internet, companies may cut down on hold times for customers with inquiries that could be answered via the website. In this respect the telephone call center and the Internet can complement each other.

Most Internet sites have e-mail links that provide one more customer service. While this does give customers the opportunity to ask individualized questions, it can provide the opportunity for service failures. Customers that communicate via e-mail are actively seeking responses to their specific questions. While the website is largely impersonal and somewhat generic, e-mail questions are not. Some studies suggest that customers expect an e-mail response faster than a voice mail message response. Some companies have found themselves faced with needing to respond to many more e-mail inquiries than their staffing would allow. Additionally, if a customer has conducted a search and has found your company as a possible provider of a product or service they are seeking, it is almost certain that they are looking at other similar companies offering similar products or services.

A customer seeking a provider of on-line stock trading services conducted a search to identify the companies that were offering this service. This search located several such providers. Two appeared to have the variety of services the customer was seeking. He then e-mailed the same set of additional questions to both companies. One company responded within three hours, apologizing for taking so long to respond. The other company took approximately four days to reply, included no explanation of why it took so long, and then provided vague answers to the questions. Who do you think that the budding investor ended up doing business with?

ENHANCING SERVICE EXPERIENCES AND BUILDING CUSTOMER LOYALTY

With all the new opportunities that await companies offering customer service, it would seem that all a company would have to do is to offer the emerging services. As we go forward into the 21st century, customers are looking for more. Customer loyalty will be one of the defining areas of success or failure for service providers. Due to the number of service providers and the diversity of services offered, customers will be exposed to a variety of different ways of serving the customer. Every service interaction is an opportunity to better understand customers and to build a relationship with them. If handled properly that relationship becomes a loyal one where customers come to think of the company as the only one for them and then continue to vote with their business.

SKILL BUILDING: TECHNOLOGY TRAINING

Technology is an important part of our lives today. Unfortunately, most Americans do not take advantage of the opportunity to maximize the technologies they already possess. Consider how many times you have purchased a new television, video cassette recorder, computer, printer, software package, camera, etc. and just started using it without reading the owner's manual. All too often the only time that we consult the owner's manual is when something will not work or breaks.

Identify a product or service that you already own or have available to you. Read the owner's manual (or specific parts) and learn how to use some feature of it that you have not previously known how to use. Now share the information with someone else who can benefit from the information. You may be surprised at how easy it is to learn a new technology when you read the instructions!

OPPORTUNITIES FOR CRITICAL THINKING

1. Describe some of the ways that customer service offerings are changing.
2. What are the three things that customers will expect from customer service providers as we enter the 21st century?
3. Review the steps to prepare others to greet new technologies with an open mind and discuss your own reaction to the introduction of new technologies.
4. Explain the difference between inbound calls and outbound calls.
5. Discuss how many times you have called a 1-800 number in the last year and your expectations of the experience.
6. Conduct and tape-record a mock telephone interview. Listen to the tape and complete a self-assessment as to whether you would be a good candidate for a call center position.
7. Conduct an Internet search and if possible e-mail a question to two companies offering a similar product or service.
8. Compare the results and share your observations with others.
9. Give examples of businesses that could benefit from a website to supplement their customer service offerings.
10. What elements do you consider to be the most important in building customer loyalty?

EXCELLENCE IN CUSTOMER SERVICE

- **EXCELLENCE IS THE GOAL**
- **GETTING STARTED**
- **REWARDS OF PROVIDING EXCELLENT CUSTOMER SERVICE**

REMEMBER THIS

Promises may get you friends, but it is performance that keeps them.
OWEN FELTHAM

EXCELLENCE IS THE GOAL

To be successful in business today requires a commitment to excellence in customer service. If excellence is the goal, anything less is not acceptable. Many companies are talking about the importance of providing excellent customer service and yet are doing little to initiate its offering. As stated in Chapter 1, one of the most effective and least expensive ways to market a business is through the provision of excellent customer service. It is not really a question of whether or not a business wants to provide customer service to its customers. Every business must provide customer service, even if they do not really want to. It has become mandatory. Customer service is exciting! If every customer is seen as a valuable asset that is difficult to replace, they are more likely to be cherished. When talking to individuals who interact with customers on a daily basis, most will tell you that an extremely fulfilling part of their job is creating positive solutions for their customers. Happy customers keep coming back to do business and to renew the relationships that they have previously established.

GETTING STARTED

Unfortunately, the main reason that more businesses are just talking about the importance of customer service and are not actually providing it is because they do not know how to get started. After reading this book and working through the skill building exercises and challenges, you have explored the fundamental requirements of creating a successful customer service program. You now know much more than the average customer service provider or customer service manager. Take the knowledge that you have acquired, both from this book and from your own experiences, and begin to offer your customers an enhanced customer experience.

REWARDS OF PROVIDING EXCELLENT CUSTOMER SERVICE

Companies that provide excellent customer service experience many rewards. Ten of the most beneficial are:

1. Customers approach business expecting a positive experience.
2. Work is more personally fulfilling.
3. Customers act as co-producers (when appropriate) in assisting in the provision of their own customer service.
4. A unique competitive edge is achieved.
5. Customer challenges are recognized and productive solutions are developed to successfully retain current customers.
6. Problems are creatively solved in an effective and efficient manner.
7. Customer service providers and management feel positive about the role that they are playing in creating positive exchanges between customers and their organization.
8. Work environments are more pleasant and productive because the value of internal customers is stressed through organization policies, procedures, and culture.

9. Businesses earn a positive reputation and the respect of customers and peers.
10. Profit goals are more successfully accomplished because business philosophies and focus are geared to satisfying customers.

The challenge of seeking and achieving excellence in customer service is not easily overcome. Equipped with the knowledge necessary to create an environment that encourages excellent customer service and the skills to successfully compete in the industry, the next step is to embark on the path of achieving individual and organizational excellence in customer service.

GLOSSARY

Brainstorming: a problem-solving strategy in which groups of two or more share ideas in an open and accepting environment. Ideas are shared with the group and recorded.

Challenging customers: those customers with problems, questions, fears, and personalities that require us to work to achieve true communication.

Churn (or Churn rate): the number of customers who leave in a year's time divided by the number of new customers in the same period.

Co-production: when customers participate in providing at least a part of their own customer service.

Communication: the process in which information, ideas, and understanding are shared between two or among more people.

Conflict: a hostile encounter that occurs as a result of opposing needs, wishes, or ideas.

Credibility: the combination of our current knowledge, reputation, and professionalism.

Culture: the values, beliefs, and norms shared by a group of people.

Customer intelligence: the process of gathering information, building a historical database, and developing an understanding of current, potential, and lapsed customers.

Customer lifetime value: the net present value of the profits a customer generates over the average customer life.

Customer retention: the continuous attempt to satisfy and keep current customers actively involved in conducting business.

Customer satisfaction: the customer's overall feeling of contentment with a customer interaction.

Customer service: anything we do for the customer that enhances the customer experience.

Customer service system: any procedure that contributes to the completion of customer service.

Defection rate: the percentage of your customers that leave you in one year.

Diagramming: a problem-solving strategy which involves creating a visual representation of a problem and system so that improvements can be made. Diagramming includes pro/con sheets, flow charts, organizational charts, and mind mapping.

Electronic mail (e-mail): Sending messages directly from one computer terminal to another. Messages may be sent and stored for later retrieval.

Empathy: the ability to understand what someone is experiencing and to take action to assist in resolving the situation.

Empowerment: to enable or permit customer service providers to make a range of decisions to assist customers.

Ethics: a set of principles that govern the conduct of an individual or group.

Expectation: our personal vision of the result that will come from our experience.

External customers: the customers we do business with outside our organization.

Eye contact: allowing our eyes to make visual contact with someone else's eyes.

Facsimile (FAX) machine: a machine that enables the transmission of graphic materials from one machine to another via telephone lines.

Flow-charts: a diagramming approach to problem solving that charts each step of a process to assist in determining why a problem is occurring. See Figure 3-3

Follow-up: checking back to determine whether or not a situation is operating according to the initial plan.

Formal leaders: those leaders who have the authority and power of their official position.

Goal: an identified result to strive to accomplish.

Goal setting: the process of establishing goals and of evaluating their importance.

High-touch customers: those customers that enter the customer experience expecting a high level of customer interaction.

Inbound calls: calls that originate with the customer that may include catalog ordering, billing questions, technical support, product use, or other information.

Informal leaders: those individuals who have no official authority, but do have the ability to influence others.

Infrastructure: the networks of people, physical facilities, and information that support the production of customer service.

Internal customers: the people we work with throughout our organization.

Job aids: leadership tools that reinforce training.

Leadership: the ability to positively influence others.

Listening: the ability to hear and understand what the speaker is saying.

Low-touch customers: those customers that enter the customer experience expecting a low level of customer interaction. Low touch frequently exists because of technology.

Market segmentation: dividing customers into groups with similar characteristics.

Mind-mapping: a creative approach to diagramming a problem, in which a problem is recorded on paper and possible solutions branch out from the original problem. See Figure 3-5

Mission: the means by which an organization will fulfill its purpose.

Motivation: the individual drive that causes us to behave in a particular way.

Needs: our personal requirements.

Negotiation: the evaluation of the possible solutions to a challenge and the selection of the solution that is mutually beneficial.

Non-Verbal: the method of communication in which the tone and inflection of one's voice, facial expressions, posture, and eye contact are used to convey or enhance a message.

Organizational charts: a method of illustrating the hierarchy of a company by illustrating who reports to whom. See Figure 3-4

Outbound calls: calls that originate from the call center to the customer, usually intended to sell products or services, conduct market research, or respond to customer inquiries.

Perception: the way we see something based on our experience.

Pitch: the highs and lows of the voice.

Planning: finding a recognizable direction to focus on and the establishment of specific customer service goals.

Primary expectations: the customer's most basic requirements of an interaction.

Pro/con sheets: a simple approach to diagramming a problem that involves recording the arguments for and against a solution. See Figure 3-2

Problem solving: an active resolution to a challenging situation.

Purpose: the reason for an organization's existence.

Reading: the ability to read and comprehend the written word.

Relationship marketing: cultivating a lasting and mutually beneficial connection with customers.

Reputation management: the process of identifying how a company is perceived and establishing an action plan to correct, maintain, or enhance their reputation.

Respect: to give someone recognition or special regard.

Responsibility check: assessing a situation and determining who should have responsibility and who really does have the responsibility.

Scope of influence: our ability to influence others based on our perceptions or experiences.

Secondary expectations: expectations based on our previous experiences that are enhancements to our primary expectations.

Self-assessment: an individual evaluation in which individual strengths and weaknesses are identified.

Self-concept: the way in which a person sees himself or herself and thinks that others see himself or herself.

Strategy: a plan for positive action.

Talking: speaking, using words and terminology that others can comprehend.

Teamwork: working together to improve the efficiency of the whole.

Teleservices: selling products and providing services or information via the telephone.

Values: a combination of our beliefs, perceptions, and ideas as to the appropriate response to a situation.

Voice inflection: a variation in the pitch, timing, or loudness of the voice.

Voice mail: a system in which a spoken message is recorded and stored in the recipient's voice mailbox. The recipient can later retrieve the audible message.

Wants: things or experiences that are desired.

Writing: communicating by using the written word so that others can understand the intended message.

Sources of Other Information

Newsletters

Customers First
Publisher: Dartnell
    4660 N. Ravenswood Avenue
    Chicago, IL 60640–4595
    1–800–621–5463 U.S.
    1–800–441–7878 Canada

Customer Service Manager's Newsletter
Publisher: Bureau of Business Practice
    24 Rope Ferry Road
    Waterford, CT 06386

Supervisor's Guide to Customer Service and Retention
Publisher: Clement Communications
    Concord Industrial Park
    Concordville, PA 19331
    1–800–345–8101

INDEX

Customer Service: A Practical Approach
Elaine Harris

Chapter 1

- **Customer service:** anything we do for the customer that enhances the customer experience.
- **Customer satisfaction:** the customer's overall feeling of contentment with a customer interaction.

- **Five needs of every customer:** service, price, quality, action, and appreciation.
- **External customers:** the customers we do business with outside our organization.
- **Internal customers:** the people we work with throughout our organization.

Chapter 2

- **Barriers to customer service:** laziness, poor communication skills, poor time management, attitude, moodiness, lack of adequate training, inability to handle stress, insufficient authority, serving customers on autopilot, and inadequate staffing.
- **Perception:** the way we see something based on our experience.
- **Expectations:** our personal vision of the result that will come from our experience.
- **Scope of influence:** our ability to influence others based on our perceptions or experiences.

- **Values:** a combination of our beliefs, perceptions, and ideas as to the appropriate response to a situation.
- **Ethics:** a set of principles that govern the conduct of an individual or group.
- **Ethics checklist:** Is it legal? Is it fair? How do I feel about it? Would the court of public opinion find me guilty? Am I fearful of what those I trust would say about my actions?

Chapter 3

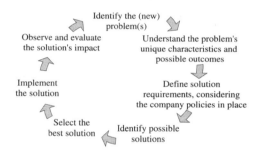

- **Problem solving model**

- **Problem solving:** an active resolution to a challenging situation.
- **Conflict:** a hostile encounter that occurs as a result of opposing needs, wishes, or ideas.
- **Problem solving strategies:** brainstorming, diagramming, organizational charts, mind mapping.
- **Follow-up:** checking back to determine whether or not a situation is operating according to the initial plan.

Chapter 4

- **Strategy:** a plan for positive action.
- **Planning:** the establishment of specific customer service goals.
- **Infrastructure:** the networks of people, physical facilities, and information that support the production of customer service.
- **Culture:** the values, beliefs, and norms shared by a group of people.
- **Examples of culture in the workplace:** Typical workday hours, industry lingo, peer accountability, levels of certification, extra company activities.
- **High-touch customers:** require a high level of customer interaction.
- **Examples of high touch:** Bank lobbies, specialty stores, hotel lobbies, purchase of real estate, lawyers and accountants, prestige restaurants.

- **Low-touch customers:** expect a low level of customer interaction.
- **Examples of low touch:** Pike passes (debit cards), automatic teller machines, express rental car checkout, hotel bill viewing on television and express checkout, pay-at-the-pump gasoline, fast food drive-up windows, do-it-yourself copy shops
- **Market segmentation:** dividing customers into groups with similar characteristics.
- **Guidelines for developing a strategy:**
  1. Segment your customers. 2. Identify the largest and most profitable customer group. 3. Determine your customers' expectations. 4. Develop a plan to efficiently achieve their expectations. 5. Implement the plan. 6. Set an evaluation timetable. 7. Evaluate and continue to improve the strategy.

Chapter 5

- **Empowerment:** to enable or permit customer service providers to make a range of decisions to assist their customers.
- **Co-production:** the customer participates in providing at least a part of his or her own service.
- **Customer service system:** any set of procedures that contributes to the completion of customer service.

- **Guidelines for system design:** 1. Identify an area in need of a new procedure or a system update. 2. List the steps necessary to create or improve the system. 3. Review the mission and purpose statement to make sure that you stay on track with the company's goals. 4. Seek to empower those involved. 5. Create a culture that supports empowerment. 6. Evaluate the system's effectiveness.

Chapter 6

- **Communication:** the process in which information, ideas, and understanding are shared between two or among more people.
- **Customer intelligence:** the process of gathering information, building a historical database, and developing an understanding of current, potential, and lapsed customers.

- **Relationship marketing:** cultivating a lasting, mutually beneficial connection with customers.
- **Words to use:** yes, please, may I consider this, do, let's negotiate.
- **Words to avoid:** can't, never, don't, you have to, don't tell me no, won't, not our policy.

Chapter 7

- **Challenging customers:** those customers with problems, questions, fears, and personalities that require us to work to achieve true communication.
- **Respect:** to give someone recognition or special regard.
- **Empathy:** the ability to understand what someone is experiencing and to take action to assist in resolving the situation.

- **Responsibility check:** assessing a situation and determining who should have responsibility and who really does have the responsibility.
- **Six super ways to cope with customers:** 1. Listen. 2. Ask questions. 3. Show empathy. 4. Solve the problem. 5. Follow up. 6. End on a positive note.

Chapter 8

- **Motivation:** the individual drive that causes us to behave in a particular way.
- **Self-concept:** the way in which a person sees himself and thinks that others see him.
- **Ten tips for improving self-concept:** 1. See yourself as a success. 2. Spend time with

positive people. 3. Eat well. Break a task down into smaller steps. 5. Get a sufficient amount of sleep. 6. Reward successes. 7. Practice positive self-talk. 8. Do something for someone else. 9. Exercise! 10. Learn something new.

Chapter 9

- **Leadership:** the ability to influence others.
- **Guidelines for praising employees:** praise in public at every opportunity; tell people what you like about them before you tell them

what you don't like; provide frequent feedback.
- **Job aids:** leadership tools that reinforce training.

Chapter 10

- **Customer retention:** the continuous attempt to satisfy and keep current customers actively involved in conducting business.
- **Churn (or churn rate):** the number of customers who leave in a year's time divided by the number of new customers in the same period. Churn = (number of defections) ÷ (number of new customers).

- **Defection rate:** the percentage of your customers that leave you in one year. Defection rate = (customers left) ÷ (customers had).
- **Customer lifetime value:** the net present value of the profits a customer generates over the average customer life. Customer lifetime value = (yearly profit) × (customer life in years).

Chapter 11

- **Teleservices:** selling products or providing services or information via the telephone.
- **Inbound calls:** calls that originate with the customer that may include catalog ordering, billing questions, technical support, product use, or other information.

- **Outbound calls:** calls that originate from the call center to the customer; usually intended to sell products or services, conduct market research, or respond to customer inquiries.

Prentice Hall
Upper Saddle River, NJ   07458

ISBN 0-13-082665-0

http://www.prenhall.com